How to Protect Everything You Own From Lawsuits and Claims

Accidents, IRS problems, unexpected medical bills, divorce, business failures or predatory lawsuit could wipe out everything you have accumulated over the years.

NOW YOU CAN FIND OUT...

- ☐ How Asset Protection can legally protect your home, savings and business from any type of lawsuit, judgment or claim

- ☐ How Asset Protection can keep you from ever getting sued

- ☐ How Asset Protection gives you the powerful leverage to make the best deal

- ☐ Why property owners are *sitting ducks* for lawsuits

- ☐ Why a living trust won't protect your property

- ☐ How to keep all of your assets completely confidential

- ☐ Why you should never be a joint-tenant

- ☐ When it is illegal to transfer your property

- ☐ The best method for saving income and estate taxes

- ☐ Why giving your property to your spouse won't protect it from claims

- ☐ What tricks investigators use to locate all of your assets

- ☐ How to set up your business to avoid liability

- ☐ Why you can be sued – *even if you never do anything wrong*

- ☐ Why Asset Protection is the best defense to a lawsuit threat

**Includes: How To Use New
LIMITED LIABILITY COMPANIES**

Published by LawTech Publishing Co., Ltd. 31921 Camino Capistrano, Suite 152, San Juan Capistrano, CA 92675-3210.

This book is sold with the understanding that neither the publisher nor the authors are engaged in offering legal or other professional advice. Any actions with regard to the information contained in this book should be undertaken only upon the advice and counsel of a trained legal professional.

Library of Congress Catalog Card Number: 94-79491

ISBN 0-915905-37-X

Printed in the United States of America

TABLE OF CONTENTS

INTRODUCTION

Several years ago a client of ours came to our office with an unusual request. He was the owner of a business which manufactured medical equipment for doctors and hospitals. He had accumulated a substantial net worth and wanted to know how he could make sure that if something went wrong in his business, he would not lose everything he had put together over the years.

Since his business was doing very well at the time, we asked him about his particular concerns and he began to list an unnerving variety of potential dangers. He felt that as a successful business owner he was a visible and attractive target for lawsuits from employees, business associates and government agencies. He was concerned about the effect of a downturn in business and was worried about what would happen if someone was injured using one of his products. These were the types of things he thought about and he wanted to know how to protect himself.

Up until that time we had never really focused on the problem of protecting assets. Our clients were mostly business owners and real estate developers whose financial concerns were limited to doing deals, making money, and saving taxes. We had never really given much thought to the question of how to hold on to assets in a dangerous business world.

As we thought about it, it seemed to us that an effective asset protection strategy involved two things. First, to the greatest extent possible, we wanted our clients to avoid getting sued in the first place. We wanted them to avoid dangerous situations that created potential liability. We felt that understanding the sources of liability and operating within the proper business structure would be effective in minimizing the lawsuit risk.

Second, and perhaps more important, we wanted to make sure that if a client were sued, despite these precautions, his personal and business assets would be protected. Our objective was to create a plan which would insulate family assets and eliminate the risk of loss from any potential liability. As an added bonus, we felt that a successful asset protection plan would, itself, eliminate the threat of most lawsuits by extinguishing the claimant's economic incentive to sue. If the other side knew that they would not be able to collect anything-even if they got a judgment-only the most irrational and foolhardy individual would willingly incur the trouble and expense of litigation. That is what we believed an effective asset protection plan would accomplish.

Our research into the issue of protecting assets from a potential judgment proved to be an exceptionally difficult problem. There was no separately published material in the law library dealing with this question. We spoke with a number of other lawyers, all experts in business law and estate planning, and none of them had any helpful suggestions for how this could be accomplished.

Finally, we began to focus on a device known as a Family Limited Partnership. This device had been used by tax lawyers for a number of years as a convenient vehicle for reducing family income taxes by shifting income from high-tax bracket parents to their children. The Family Limited Partnership was also extremely useful as a technique for dramatically reducing estate taxes on family wealth as it passed from parents to their children. But to us, the most exciting discovery was that the Family Limited Partnership was an especially well suited mechanism for protecting personal assets from a potential judgment. We found that when properly structured, the arrangement allowed a husband and wife to transfer their home, savings, and business interests into a protected form while maintaining complete control over the assets. Yet, if somebody successfully sued either the husband or the wife, that person would not be able to seize the assets in the Family Limited Partnership.

After substantial additional research and discussion, we began to create asset protection plans for our clients, using the Family Limited Partnership as the centerpiece of these plans. Our experience has been that when these partnerships are combined with a device known as an Asset Protection Trust, the most powerful and sophisticated asset protection can be accomplished.

Over the last year, in particular, we have seen the interest in asset protection reach significant proportions. Almost every major business journal and magazine has published articles about the topic and two of the leading legal publishers have produced full legal textbooks on the subject. In response to what has now become an overwhelming demand, a growing number of attorneys throughout the country are now setting up these types of asset protection plans for their clients. But up until now, there has been virtually no published material available for either laymen or lawyers which specifically discusses the various asset protection techniques and how they can be accomplished.

This book is our effort to provide a wider public understanding of the problem and to offer the solutions which we have developed. In Chapters One, Two and Three, we show you the reasons why people get sued and what happens if you are involved in a lawsuit. Chapter Four gives a preview of developing an asset protection plan. Chapter Five discusses the legal limitations on transferring assets which are considered to be "Fraudulent Transfers." Chapters, Six, Seven, Eight and Nine contain a discussion of the different legal arrangements that are used in creating an asset protection plan, covering the use of corporations, trusts, gifts, and partnerships. Chapter Ten summarizes the overall procedure for creating an asset protection plan.

Appendix A provides a discussion of Limited Liability Companies, a new and extremely favorable development in almost every state. Appendix B provides a more detailed discussion of a number of asset protection issues, including case citations and statutes where appropriate. We have chosen to separate this material from the basic text in order to avoid diminishing the readability of the book, while still providing sufficient detail for those who wish to pursue the subject in greater depth. Appendix C is devoted to Questions and Answers which we hope will pull together the most important ideas from the material.

As a word of caution, this book cannot possibly substitute for competent legal advice. Our treatment of the law is general and is not intended as a comprehensive discussion of all relevant issues. The law in each state will vary to some extent and the applicability of the law will depend upon your individual circumstances. If you have a particular question about the information in this book, you can telephone us at (800) 223-4291 and we will try our best to help you.

WHY YOU NEED ASSET PROTECTION

THE LITIGATION EXPLOSION

It has been estimated that 50,000 lawsuits are filed in this country every day of the week. This has come to be known as the "litigation explosion." Whatever the causes - a breakdown of traditional values, the loss of a sense of community, too many hungry lawyers, wasteful insurance companies-the impact on each of us is significant.

When patients sue doctors, the cost of health care rises. To compensate for product liability claims, manufacturers add a premium to the price of their products. Litigation cripples business. It is time consuming, expensive and emotionally charged. It detracts from our ability to focus on productive issues, as attention is directed away from matters of efficiency and innovation. Parties to a lawsuit spend so much time meeting with lawyers and fighting with the other side that nothing gets accomplished. As businesses are dragged under by the burdens of litigation our whole society suffers.

If you are engaged in any business activity or if you have a professional practice, chances are that sooner or later you will be sued. And if you are sued, everything that you have worked hard to create will be placed in jeopardy. The costs of defending even a frivolous suit can easily reach $50,000 to $100,000. Once you get to court, you will find that the system is heavily weighted toward the sympathetic plaintiff, as judges and juries play Robin Hood with your money. These judges and juries are continually expanding theories of liability and stratospheric damage and punitive damage awards are now routine. It is no longer uncommon for awards in negligence cases to exceed $1,000,000.

Our legal system should hold people responsible for their acts. If someone causes injury that person should be required to fairly compensate the victim for his loss. Not many people would seriously object to this principle. The problem is that this general principle bears no relationship to what is actually occurring in the legal system today.

THE DEEP POCKET DEFENDANT

The reality of our legal system is that people are named as defendants in lawsuits not because of their degree of fault but because of their ability to pay. When an attorney is approached by a potential client who is claiming injury or economic loss, the attorney will consider whether a theory of liability can be developed against a party who can pay a judgment. This is called the search for the "Deep Pocket Defendant."

The Deep Pocket Defendant will have substantial insurance coverage or significant personal assets. The measure of an attorney's skill is his ability to create a theory of liability which will connect a Deep Pocket Defendant to the facts of a particular case.

Here is an example of how an attorney might approach a particular case:

Mr. Woodrow is driving in his car. Mr. Fishbrain runs through a stop sign at an intersection, smashing into Woodrow's car and causing Woodrow severe injury.

From his hospital bed, Woodrow looks through the Yellow Pages and calls the first attorney he sees, the famous Alan Aardvark.

Aardvark is what is known as a "Contingent Fee" lawyer. He will work for a percentage of the ultimate recovery. He determines whether to invest his time and money in a case based upon what his expected return will be. Since the time and expense of preparing for litigation can be considerable an attorney cannot afford to take a case that is not likely to pay off. You have heard these guys on television. No Recovery-No Fee. The deal is usually that the attorney advances all costs and expenses and in exchange he recovers these costs plus 30% to 40% of any amounts which he can get from the defendant.

Accordingly, before Aardvark decides to take Woodrow's case he will want to do some investigation. He will want to know whether Fishbrain has substantial assets in order to make the case worthwhile. We will discuss in greater detail later the techniques which a lawyer uses to find out what assets you own.

For right now let's assume that Aardvark quickly determines that Fishbrain has no insurance and no significant assets such as a home or a retirement nest-egg. So what happens now? Is that the end of the case?

As for Fishbrain it probably is the end of the case. Even though Fishbrain was clearly responsible, Aardvark is not going to waste his time suing someone who can't pay. But Aardvark is not going to give up so easily. He has a client with substantial injuries and that means Big Bucks. He has to find someone who can pay. And if he is going to make some money on this case, he will have to be creative.

Here is how he will analyze the case to try to draw in a Deep Pocket Defendant.

1. Was Fishbrain on an errand for his employer at the time of the crash? If so maybe we can sue the employer.

2. Did Fishbrain have any alcohol in his system? Possible case against the restaurant that served him.

3. Was Fishbrain on any medication? Possible case against the pharmacist or drug company for inadequate warning label.

4. The stop sign Fishbrain ran through was in a residential neighborhood in front of someone's house. Check to see whether the homeowners foliage obstructed the view of the stop sign. If so, there is a possible case against the homeowner for negligence.

5. The driver's side door of Woodward's car collapsed on impact. Possible case against the manufacturer for not making a more crash resistant frame.

Do you see how far we are moving away from Fishbrain-the person responsible for the accident-in an effort to tie in a remote Deep Pocket Defendant?

The example that I just gave you is taken from a real case. Guess who ended up as the defendant.

In the actual case the defendant was Fishbrain's 92 year old widowed great aunt. As it turned out, she had purchased the car for Fishbrain as a gift to him. She was named as the defendant in the case and was found liable on a theory called Negligent Entrustment. The jury found that she should not have bought the car for her grand-nephew because she should have known he would cause an accident. The verdict was for $932,000, and Fishbrain's great aunt lost everything she owned.

The point of all this is that the foundation of every lawsuit is a defendant who can pay. Once such a defendant is located, it is easy enough to construct a theory of why that defendant should be responsible. Judges and juries often act on their emotions—not on the law. And when the contest is between an injured or a sympathetic plaintiff against a wealthy or *comparatively* wealthy defendant, the plaintiff will win virtually every time, regardless of the defendant's actual degree of fault.

As a result, the plaintiff's attorney will search for a party who can pay a hefty judgment. In the old days it was said that *"He who has the gold makes the rules."* Now the saying goes *"He who has the gold pays the plaintiff."* The fact is that no matter how remote your connection to an injury, if you have even modest assets, an attorney for the injured party will attempt to show that you are somehow legally at fault and you will be named as a defendant in the case.

The Property Owner

Anyone who owns property is a potential Deep Pocket Defendant. Assume you own a small apartment building. One evening a female tenant returns home from work and parks her car in the enclosed parking garage. As she gets out of her car, she is raped and robbed by an assailant. Under these circumstances, you can expect a lawsuit against you as the owner of the property, for negligently failing to provide the proper level of security.

Regardless of the actual safety measures which you employ, the plaintiff's attorney will allege that you should have taken additional steps, such as installing video cameras, floodlights, or hiring security guards to protect the safety of the tenants. In essence, as a property owner and a Deep Pocket Defendant, you become a guarantor of the safety of your tenants, to the full extent of your available net worth.

Officers and Directors

Officers and directors of publicly traded companies are also popular Deep Pocket Defendants. All companies whose shares are publicly traded must file quarterly and annual reports with the Securities and Exchange Commission. These reports are known respectively as the 10-Q and 10-K filings. The purpose of these filings is to make information concerning the business and finances of the company publicly available. The law requires that public companies provide full disclosure of all material information which may influence the price of its stock.

A number of law firms employ young MBA's and attorneys to scrutinize each of the required filings made by these companies. If the stock of a company rises or falls sharply in response to some news item affecting the company, a law firm may attempt to show that the company's filings failed to adequately disclose certain material information. If any possible claim can be made, a class action lawsuit will be filed on behalf of current or former shareholders. The company, its officers and directors will be named in the suit. The defendants will fight the lawsuit or settle it but in either event the cost will be substantial and the only likely winners will be the lawyers who filed the action.

HIGH RISK OCCUPATIONS

In addition to potential liability as a Deep Pocket Defendant, certain types of businesses create a high degree of lawsuit exposure.

Physicians

All physicians are acutely sensitive to the risk of lawsuits. A recent study found that between 70 and 80 percent of all obstetricians had been sued. Neurosurgeons and other medical specialists are also frequent targets. It seems that the public now perceives doctors, like auto mechanics, as capable of fixing any problem with the right tools and a good supply of parts. When these unreasonable expectations are not met—when a surgery or procedure is not successful—the patient and his family conclude that the only explanation is that the doctor must have been at fault. It is not fate, or nature, or an act of God which is blamed for the misfortune. (It is much too difficult to collect a judgment from these parties.) As a result, many doctors have been forced to significantly narrow the scope of their practice to eliminate even modestly risky procedures. This type of defensive medicine inevitably drives up health care costs for everyone.

Real Estate Developers

Real estate developers and construction companies are another group with potentially significant personal liability. When a project is developed and sold, there may be liability to purchasers and subsequent purchasers for many years to come. Damages caused by latent (unseen) construction defects may be either uninsurable or may surface only after a policy has expired. As an example, California law states that a builder remains legally responsible for latent defects for up to ten years after the completion of the building. With potential liability having a "tail" of up to ten years, no builder is immune from a crippling lawsuit which may have been caused by the faulty workmanship of a subcontractor who has long since disappeared.

The recent decline in real estate prices has also spurred a rash of lawsuits against developers and general contractors. Homeowners who have lost a significant amount of equity due to depressed market conditions often attempt to recover their investment by filing lawsuits, alleging construction defects against everyone involved in the project. That includes the geologists, engineers, architects and the building trades people as well as the developer. These types of cases are enormously costly and time consuming to defend and unless there is an insurance company involved to pay the costs, it is very difficult for all but the largest companies to survive a lawsuit like this.

Another problem faced by developers is that each project requires a significant amount of cash, most of which is borrowed from a lending institution. The developer puts up the land as security and also must sign a personal guarantee for the entire amount. If the deal goes bad, the developer must repay the loan out of his own pocket. As a result, one bad deal can wipe out many years of hard work.

Because of the high degree of risk associated with these types of business activities, the owners of these businesses are placing their entire net worth in jeopardy every single day. Each time a doctor performs surgery, he is literally betting the house on a successful outcome. Anytime something goes wrong, someone will sue. Every patient, client or customer is a potential legal adversary.

GENERAL BUSINESS RISKS

In addition to the degree of risk associated with particular business activities, there is a significant threat of personal liability due to general business risks. This type of potential liability exists regardless of the degree of hazard associated with the activities of the business. This is the liability which any business incurs in connection with obligations to lenders, landlords, suppliers and customers.

Almost every business needs to borrow money at one time or another for operating capital, inventory or equipment. It is anticipated that the money will be repaid out of future cash flow. The problem arises when this cash flow falls short of expectations, because of an error in judgment, an unforeseen slowdown in business or because of one or two unlucky breaks.

In April, 1992, there was an accident in Chicago that caused water from the Chicago River to pour into underground tunnels in the center of the downtown area. Hundreds of buildings were flooded, power was shut down and businesses were temporarily closed. Many of these small businesses did not survive this incident. Expenses, such as interest, rent and overhead continued even though revenue for the period was lost forever. Very few businesses have sufficient cash reserves to withstand these disastrous circumstances.

As the recent riots in Los Angeles have painfully illustrated, many of the small shopkeepers were either uninsured or underinsured. In many cases, those people have lost everything. Even those shopkeepers who were fully insured for the contents of their stores were unable to pay rent during the rebuilding period. This created a chain reaction in which the shopkeeper's landlord could not pay his mortgage because of his tenants inability to pay him. For those few who were fortunate enough to have had full replacement and business interruption insurance, the future may prove to be less kind. Many insurance companies in high risk areas will eliminate coverage completely, leaving every store owner without protection from normally insurable business risks.

The point is that there are hundreds of ways to get wiped out in business: a general economic downturn; shortages due to a business upturn; sudden changes in the public's taste; the emergence of powerful, well financed competitors; the obsolescence of products due to the invention of new or more appealing products; or a change in the law. The next thing you know, your banker and your landlord and your suppliers are fighting over who should get your house and how to divide up the china. The worst part is that these risks are uncontrollable. No matter how smart and how careful you may be, no one has the ability to foresee all of the things that will go wrong.

Consider the case of the Mr. and Mrs. Smith. Mr. Smith is 50 years old, and owns a small advertising agency from which he draws a salary of $75,000. Mrs. Smith is 48, and an editor of a local newspaper. She makes $50,000 per year. They have two teenage children. Over the years they have managed to accumulate equity in their home of $50,000 plus savings of $75,000 for their retirement and for their children's education. By living frugally, they anticipate that each year they will be able to put aside an additional $5,000 for their nest egg.

One day Mr. Smith gets a big break. He finally lands a huge new account for his advertising agency which promises to double the firms revenue. The client is Home National Savings, the largest savings and loan in town. The fees from this account will provide Mr. Smith with substantially greater income and retirement savings.

In order to handle all of this new work Mr. Smith hires three more employees and signs a lease for more space in a nearby office building. The landlord offers him very attractive terms if he will sign a ten year lease and Mr. Smith agrees.

The terms of the new lease require Mr. Smith to make rental payments of $5,000 per month for the ten year period. This amount is triple what he had been paying but with the additional income from the new account he considers this to be a reasonable amount.

During the next year everything goes according to plan. The Smith's manage to save over $25,000. They even take a two week vacation in the Caribbean and still have $100,000 in their savings account.

A month later Mr. Smith reads in the newspaper that Home National Savings has been taken over by the RTC. He receives notification in the mail to stop all work on the account. Mr. Smith lays off all of the new employees he hired for the account and he contacts his landlord to see if he can move out of his space.

Mr. Smith's landlord informs him that he cannot possibly let him out of the lease. The real estate market has softened considerably and the demand for office space is very low. The landlord tells him that the remaining nine year balance of the lease payments is $540,000 and he expects to get paid the full rent every month.

Mr. Smith's choices are now very limited. If he walks away from the lease he will be sued by the landlord for the entire $540,000, plus attorneys fees. Under every lease the landlord has the right to sue for the full amount of the lease if any payments are not met.

Alternatively, Mr. Smith could remain in the space and continue to make the payments, hoping that he will land another large account before he has exhausted all of the family retirement savings.

We can see that either option places at risk everything that the Smith family has accumulated over the years. Did Mr. Smith make a foolish decision when he decided to take on the new client?

The fact is that every business and financial decision which you make entails some level of risk. If you try to make more money by expanding your business, or making a new investment with the goal of ultimately increasing your financial security, you will necessarily jeopardize everything that you have earned up until that point. Sometimes everything will work out as you hope it will, but sometimes it won't.

We will see that the point of Asset Protection is to allow you to engage in business and take the necessary risks, while making sure that if things do no go as planned, everything that you have put together over the years will not be lost.

Before we get to our discussion of what you can do to protect yourself from all of this, we need to briefly cover some of the other legal sources of potential liability.

WHY YOU WILL PROBABLY GET SUED

In addition to risks faced by all business owners, it is important to understand the particular types of liability which arise out of various commercial and personal relationships.

DANGEROUS CONTRACTS

Oral Contracts

A contract is formed any time two people make an agreement to do, or not to do something. Certain types of contracts, involving commercial transactions must be in writing in order to be valid. But most contracts do not have to be written.

A promise that you make is considered to be a contract if the other party relies on your promise. Recently, we have seen girlfriends and boyfriends claim that they were promised certain things by their former mates. These alleged promises called for lifetime care and support or a specific dollar amount to be paid at the end of the relationship. Since, by its nature, an oral agreement has no visible trail, these cases come down to one person's word against the other.

One interesting case that we have seen involved the ownership of a California lottery ticket. A man and woman lived together but weren't married. He was elderly and she took care of him. They kept some spare change and a few dollars in a coffee can in the kitchen. The woman would take out a dollar every few days to buy a lottery ticket. Over the years, there were a few winning tickets worth $20 or $100 and those amounts would go back into the coffee can to finance future tickets.

One day they hit the grand prize of $12,000,000—twenty annual payments of $600,000, less taxes. Naturally, the man claimed that the money in the coffee can was his money and he was the sole owner of the ticket. She claimed that they had always treated that money as joint property and that she was entitled to half of the winnings.

The case went to trial in San Diego in June 1992 and the jury found that there was no agreement between the parties to share the winnings. The entire amount belonged to the man.

We certainly do not know who was telling the truth, and that's exactly the point. Nobody ever knows for sure who is telling the truth in these situations. That is why anyone with whom you are involved, in any kind of business or personal relationship, can claim that you broke a promise and that they are entitled to some amount of compensation.

An employee can claim that you promised him a job for life. Let's say that you own a business and you decide that the work of John Jones, one of your senior employees, is no longer satisfactory. If you fire Mr. Jones there is an excellent chance that he will sue you. In the lawsuit he will claim that he is entitled to a percentage of ownership in your company based upon an oral agreement which you made.

That is all he needs to do. He doesn't need any other evidence. He simply claims that you made certain promises and now you have to defend yourself and risk losing a portion of your business. It is now your word against his and the jury can decide who they believe. These types of claims are made every day in our courts and many employers end up making huge settlements with the fired employee in order to avoid the expense of litigation and the risk of loss.

A Japanese chip manufacturer in the Silicon Valley closed down its plant and laid off all the workers. The company was sued by all 868 workers for over one billion dollars on the grounds that they were promised lifetime employment. The case was ultimately settled for over $20,000,000 after millions of dollars in legal fees and thousands of hours of wasted time and energy.

Claims of a contract based upon an oral agreement are very difficult to defend against. It is simply not practical to write out a contract, specifying the terms of the relationship with each person you meet. Everyone faces enormous potential liability for these kinds of claims.

Loans

A loan is also a type of contract. The terms are usually set forth in a written "promissory note." A failure to make payments according to the loan terms is a violation of the contract. Loans may be either "secured" or "unsecured." When you secure a loan the lender will generally have a recorded interest, such as a mortgage on real estate that you own.

When a loan is secured by property other than real estate, the lender will publicly record a lien on the property securing the debt. This type of document is known as a UCC Financing Statement.

If you default on the loan, the lender will "foreclose" on the property securing the loan. If the auction sale price is less than the balance of the loan, the lender may be able to get a deficiency judgment against you to recover the balance.

In the past, real estate was an appreciating asset and the value of the property was generally sufficient to repay the balance of the loan in the event of foreclosure. Deficiencies were an unusual occurrence. Lately, with real estate prices flat or declining in many areas, deficiency judgments have become more typical in foreclosure situations.

When a loan is unsecured, the lender will first obtain a judgment by a court and then attempt to collect from you by seizing any personal assets which you own. This procedure for collection is described in Chapter Three.

Leases

Leases are another type of contract that represent a source of potential liability. When you lease office or retail space for your business, you are entering into a contract to make payments for a number of years. If you fail to make the payments, the landlord will have the right to evict you and obtain a judgment for the remaining payments. If you enter into a ten year lease, but can't make payments after the first year, you will still owe the landlord nine years of rent.

The landlord is under a duty to reduce (or "mitigate") his damages by attempting to re-rent the space. Any amount which he is able to recover by obtaining a new tenant will reduce the amount of your obligation. If your lease provided for rent of $20,000 per year and the landlord re-rents the space for $15,000 per year, you will be liable only for this difference. During periods of escalating rents and low vacancy rates liability for leases is not a significant problem. If you cannot make the payments, you can usually sublet to another tenant. But when rents are declining and vacancy rates are high, a lease obligation becomes a serious and dangerous source of liability.

Purchases and Sales of Goods

Purchases of goods and equipment from suppliers and sales of goods to customers are also governed by contract law. A contract with vendors or customers is usually in the form of a purchase order or invoice. The terms of the contract are in the small print on the form.

When you purchase a product, you are liable to the seller for the purchase price of the goods. When you sell a product, the law creates a warranty between you and your customer that the product is fit for its intended purpose.

Disputes sometimes arise about the quality of the merchandise. You may claim that you ordered red shirts and the supplier says you ordered green shirts. He wants you to pay but you want to return the shipment. These types of fights may end up in a lawsuit.

In Chapter Six we will discuss the use of corporations and we will see the extent to which personal liability can be reduced when entering into these kinds of contracts.

NEGLIGENCE
Looking For Someone To Blame

In addition to liability for contracts, individuals and businesses face potential lawsuits for negligence. You will be considered to be negligent if a party is injured or his property is damaged because of your failure to exercise reasonable care. This is known as direct negligence. You may also be sued when you are legally responsible for the wrongful acts of others, such as a child or an employee. This type of liability is known as imputed negligence.

Direct Negligence

Direct negligence is exemplified by hitting someone while driving your car unsafely. The death of a patient due to a physician's diagnosis which fell short of the advice of the hypothetical "common physician" is another example of direct negligence. An attorney's advice to his client which is based upon a faulty understanding of the law or which falls short of the legal standard of proper investigation and diligence is also a matter of direct negligence. In other words, if, in the conduct of your business, you act in a way that is less then the minimum standard of performance the law requires for your job, then you are guilty of negligence and you will be liable for all foreseeable consequences of your careless acts.

Negligence can occur because of your *failure to act* as well as your improper acts. Failing to move to the side of the road when you hear an ambulance coming up behind you is negligent. A physician's failure to prescribe a recognized treatment is negligent. The attorney's failure to advice a client of the law relevant to the particular situation is negligence.

Imputed Negligence

In certain situations, you may be held liable for an injury even if you are not directly at fault. Imputed negligence means that the law will hold you responsible for the negligence of someone else. A negligent act by an employee, conducted in the scope of his employment, will be imputed to the employer. If you ask your secretary to pick up some sandwiches for lunch, she is acting within the scope of her employment when she drives to the deli. If she is at fault in an automobile accident, her negligence is imputed to you. You are responsible for the damages caused by her acts.

Expanded Theories

In recent years, courts, state legislators and clever trial attorneys have dramatically expanded traditional theories of negligence. As stated, negligence means a failure to exercise the proper degree of care. The question is *what is the proper degree of care?* How careful must we be?

A famous rock group was sued awhile ago by the parents of a teenage boy who was terribly injured when his suicide attempt failed. The parents claimed that the boy had been encouraged to commit the act by listening to certain lyrics on a record album. Although it was ultimately determined that the group was not liable for the boy's death, the case did make it all the way through trial. The members of the group sat through countless hours of depositions and testimony and surely spent several hundred thousand dollars in legal fees. All of this time and money was wasted, because an attorney for the boy's parents attempted to connect a remote Deep Pocket Defendant to the case in order to obtain compensation for this unfortunate, but blameless event.

Take this example. Meticulous Max noticed that the brakes on his car were not working properly. Feeling the car was unsafe to drive, on Monday, Max made an appointment for his mechanic to pick up the vehicle in a tow truck on Wednesday. Late Monday night the car was stolen. As the thief was driving away in the car, the brakes failed and he crashed into another vehicle. The person driving the other car, Bob Brown, was injured in the accident. Bob sued Max alleging that Max was negligent in failing to properly maintain his automobile. Because of the high incidence of stolen cars, Max "should have" reasonably foreseen that his car might be stolen and, if stolen, the faulty brakes would likely cause injury to someone. On this theory, Bob was successful and was awarded $325,000 by the jury. Clearly, Max thought he was exercising due care by not driving his car and by arranging for an appointment to have the brakes fixed. However, the jury expanded the concept of "due care" ruling that Max acted improperly by agreeing to wait two days to have his car repaired.

This leaves us with a legally required standard of behavior that cannot be ascertained in advance. (And with which most people in Max's town would disagree.) We know we have to be careful but we do not know what that means. It is impossible to anticipate what standard a jury will impose with the advantage of hindsight. That is the problem.

THE PROBLEM WITH EMPLOYEES

Another area of the law that has been expanding dramatically in recent years involves the relationship between employers and employees. According to a recent study, California courts have been deluged with more than 100,000 employee lawsuits for wrongful termination, sexual harassment or employment discrimination. Employers who give a departing employee a bad reference are often sued for defamation or a related theory.

According to Walter K. Olson, author of "The Litigation Explosion", studies have shown that employer-defendants lost 78% of the time in cases decided by a jury with an average award of $424,527. The average award in a wrongful dismissal case was found to be $646,000 and the average age discrimination verdict was $722,000.

Wrongful termination may be alleged by an employee who was fired or an employee who has had his work responsibilities severely altered. The latter case is known as a constructive termination. As noted previously, companies which close down a factory have been sued for wrongful termination on behalf of all of the employees. Any employee who is fired, regardless of his actual work performance, can claim that he was wrongfully terminated, in violation of a written or oral agreement or understanding between the employee and the company.

Employment discrimination involves discriminatory practices in hiring, firing, promotions and salary with regard to particular classes of employees. Discrimination based upon race or sex is a violation of the law. In several recent cases, employees have received multi-million dollar jury awards, including punitive damages. Recently, a woman was awarded $20,000,000 by a jury for sex discrimination in a suit against Texaco. Another woman received $3,100,000 in a similar case against a San Diego company.

THE BIG FOOT
OF THE GOVERNMENT

Every aspect of daily business life is inextricably tied to some form of government regulation.

Everyone is aware of the liability for corporate and individual income taxes. Anyone who has tangled with the IRS over an income tax deficiency knows how difficult it can be to work themselves out of the bureaucratic nightmare that is created once the IRS begins any collection process.

Recently, the IRS has focused its audit procedures on the issue of independent contractors versus employee status. In order to avoid payroll withholding and the employer's share of withholding taxes, many companies treat as independent contractors certain individuals performing services for the company. Often, this treatment is standard within a particular industry and one company cannot compete with others in the business if it is forced to pay payroll taxes on its workers. For example, in the trucking industry it is common for truck owners to hire drivers who are treated as independent contractors.

On audit, the IRS usually takes the position that these persons were really employees, not independent contractors. If the IRS prevails on this issue, the employer is liable for a 100% penalty equal to the amount of income taxes and social security taxes which should have been withheld. This amount is a liability not only of the company, but also of the officers and directors of the company. The IRS can look to the officers and directors for the entire payment of this amount. This potentially enormous liability hangs over the head of every business owner who treats his workers as independent contractors and fails to withhold payroll taxes on their income.

Federal, state, and local agencies, including the SEC, and the Environmental Protection Agency have the power to assess civil penalties for failure to comply with specific regulations. A client who operated a gas station was ordered to undertake a complex and costly cleanup of toxic material beneath his property, caused by a prior owner and not previously known to him. These types of surprise liabilities often have a devastating financial impact because they have not been anticipated in the budget and funds to meet these obligations are often not available.

BEATING UP THE COMPETITION

Litigation has become a tool to savage the competition. Take, for example, the story reported in the May 12, 1992 Investors Business Daily concerning the tactics of Intel Corp., the largest semi-conductor chip maker in the United States, against Cyrix Corp., a tiny upstart formed in 1988. The day after Cyrix introduced a new chip which was both faster and cheaper than Intel's chip, Intel filed a patent infringement lawsuit. Cyrix officials claimed that the lawsuit was filed even before Intel had the opportunity to examine the Cyrix chip to verify whether its patent had, in fact, been violated. With obvious disgust and frustration, the President of Cyrix, Jerry Rogers, was quoted as saying: "I thought we could pursue the American Dream and let the market decide who is best. Too much money is being spent on lawyers and not enough on R & D (research and development). Intel has no downside for pursuing us in court. In the end they will lose, but I am having to spend a lot of time talking about this litigation when I could be talking to customers."

Mr. Rogers is certainly not alone in his complaint. Lawsuits are a standard tactic in business in order to bury weaker competition. Complex litigation is so expensive, that large companies can literally destroy their smaller opposition. The money spent by the large companies on this type of litigation is considered by them to be a good investment, since these amounts will ultimately be less than the amount it would cost them to compete fairly based on the price and quality of their products.

PAYING YOUR PARTNER'S DEBTS

Partnerships

It may surprise you to know that you are responsible and liable for the acts of your partner. The Uniform Partnership Act says that a partner is liable for any obligations created by his partner on behalf of the partnership, even if the innocent partner knew nothing whatsoever about his partner's deeds.

For example, if your partner and co-owner of an ice-cream store, John Vanilla, in an act of unbridled optimism, orders an additional twenty gallons of butter-pecan ice-cream from your supplier, you will be personally liable for writing the check out of your own account if neither the business nor John can pay the invoice. The same would be true if John ordered a new gelato maker for $50,000. If John doesn't pay, the whole amount is your obligation.

This joint liability is not limited to contracts. You will also be liable for any personal injuries caused by your partner in the conduct of your partnership's business. For example, in a medical partnership of two or more doctors, each is responsible for injuries caused by the other's malpractice. Similarly, if one partner goes out to buy office supplies and injures someone with his car, all partners are legally responsible for the damages.

This legal concept that both ("joint") and each ("several") of you are liable for the payment of the business's debts is a well established, but frequently unknown risk. This may be in part, because *between the partners themselves*, each of them is responsible for their designated share of debts of the partnership. In other words, any one partner can demand that his co-partners pay their ownership share for all business expenses.

This right of "contribution" is, however, more often illusory than real. Take this example: Five people get together to open an antique furniture store. Each owns 20% of the business, receives 20% of the profits and pays 20% of the expenses. The first large shipment of furniture is ordered, a lease is signed and sales people are hired. Six months later the business is "belly up" and the business debts amount to $1,000,000. If you are one of the partners you may be operating under the mistaken belief that you are only responsible for $200,000 or 20% of the total partnership debt. If your partners cannot or will not pay their share, you may then sue them to force them to contribute their share of the total amount. In the not-so-unusual case, your creditors will sue you for the payment of the entire $1,000,000, three of your partners will declare bankruptcy, and the other partner will have no assets of which to speak. Lo and behold, you will be left alone - holding the bag.

Co-Tenants

Closely related to the partnership scenario is the relationship known as a co-tenancy. You may be involved in a co-tenancy today, even though you do not know it. A co-tenancy exists any time two or more people share ownership of a property. Ownership of a house as joint-tenants or tenants-in-common are examples of co-tenancy relationships. As a co-tenant you have joint and several liability for the acts of your co-tenant, the same as in a partnership.

A client sought our advice about an office lease that he shared with a friend. They believed that rather than signing separate leases, they would save rent and improve their business environment by leasing one large suite and dividing the offices between them. So they both signed the lease for the entire suite for a five year term. Each took one-half of the space and agreed to pay one-half of the rent. Within the first year, our client's friend faced severe business problems which forced him into a personal bankruptcy. Our client faithfully continued to pay his 50% share of the rent directly to the landlord. You can imagine his surprise when the landlord sued him for the 50% of the rent that was not being paid on his friend's space. Incredulous he came to us to ask if he really could be held legally responsible for the portion of the office that he did not use. The answer was that as a co-tenant he had joint and several liability with the other tenant and that he was, indeed, personally liable for his friend's share of the rent on the suite.

NEVER BE A DIRECTOR

Serving on the board of directors of a corporation, bank or charitable organization has long been regarded as a prestigious honor bestowed on virtuous business and civic leaders in the community. Lately, this honor has turned out not to be such an honor after all. That is because the directors of these organizations are now routinely named in lawsuits by disgruntled shareholders, employees, and government agencies.

Almost every major decision reached by a board of directors may be the source of a potential lawsuit. A board of directors is responsible for the overall management of a company. Day to day operations are carried out by the officers of the corporation, but the board is responsible for major decisions affecting the rights of the shareholders. The board has a fiduciary obligation to act in the best interests of the shareholders.

During the takeover craze of the last ten years, directors were forced to consider buy-out offers from management or outside groups. Usually, the offers far exceeded the current price for the stock. Should the offer be accepted or should the board hold out for a higher bid? What if they held out for a higher bid and the initial offer was withdrawn? The members of the board were usually in a no win position. Either way, there loomed a lawsuit claiming that the board breached its fiduciary obligations to the shareholders.

Many who have served on the board of directors of local banks and savings and loans have done so to their everlasting regret. Failed institutions have been taken over by the Resolution Trust Corporation (RTC) or other organizations created by Congress. The RTC now routinely files lawsuits against all prior members of the failed institution's board of directors charging them with negligence in overseeing the savings and loans' operations. Certainly, some of these directors engaged in fraudulent and self-serving dealings. But more often than not, the RTC's broad net catches many decent and honest citizens who performed their jobs with reasonable skill and care. Those individuals are now being financially devastated by the legal expenses of defending against the RTC onslaught.

The conclusion is inescapable. If you are a member of a board of directors, you are a visible target defendant. If you are ever asked to sit on a board, just don't do it.

WHAT HAPPENS IN A LAWSUIT

In this Chapter we will discuss what happens in a typical lawsuit. To illustrate, we will use a hypothetical involving a fictitious Mr. John Williams. Williams is an author who recently completed a detailed investigative study of a particular religious sect. After the book was published, the leader of the sect filed a lawsuit against Williams for defamation. The sect has a reputation for attempting to intimidate and coerce anyone who might reveal damaging information about the group and the major weapon in this intimidation process is the use of lawsuits. (That is why we are not mentioning their name.)

A lawsuit has five separate stages:

    (1) Economic analysis of the case

    (2) The pleadings

    (3) Discovery

    (4) Trial

    (5) Collection

ECONOMIC ANALYSIS; ARE YOU WORTH SUING?

Before any lawsuit is commenced, the claimant (the plaintiff) and his attorney will review the economics of the case. The plaintiff will weigh the costs of prosecuting the case against the likelihood of victory and the amount of the probable recovery.

Plaintiff's Cost to Sue You

Hourly Attorney

The costs involved in suing someone depend primarily on whether the attorney is working on an hourly rate or a contingency fee. Most, but not all, cases concerning business disputes are handled on an hourly basis. Typically, these hourly fees range from $100 to $375 per hour. Legal fees in pursuing a garden variety case to trial can be $50,000 to $100,000. In a case of some complexity, the legal fees can easily reach $1,000,000.

An hourly fee attorney has an economic stake in encouraging the litigation. Since the attorney gets paid his hourly rate, regardless of the outcome, there is a huge incentive for the attorney to "sell" the case to his client. The lawyer will encourage the client to sue in order to generate substantial fees for himself. (The next time you are encouraged by an hourly fee attorney to file a lawsuit, try asking him if he will take the case on a contingency.)

The attorney's inherent incentive to litigate discourages early reasonable settlements between the parties. We have seen over and over again in our practice that it is nearly impossible to get an attorney to devote his attention to an early and reasonable settlement. Instead, the lawyers generally adopt severe and inflexible negotiating positions while attempting to persuade their client that the *other* side is unreasonable. Cases are usually not settled early in the process unless the client is particularly sophisticated and understands his attorney's financial interest in pursuing the litigation.

If the case is not settled early, it is almost always settled late-when the client's resources or patience (or both) are nearly exhausted. Usually this occurs just prior to trial - *after* the client has already spent substantial sums and he finds out what the additional fees will be if a trial is necessary. At this point attorneys for both sides get very reasonable in their demands. Whatever it takes, a settlement is reached at this point. That is why only about 1% of all the lawsuits that are filed ever get to trial.

Several years ago we represented a well known professional athlete in a case against his former financial advisor. The financial advisor "sold" our client on a real estate investment by seriously misrepresenting the important facts about the deal. Our client had lost $100,000 and wanted his money back.

The other side (let's call him Mr. Jones) was represented by a large prestigious West Coast law firm. They were being paid on an hourly basis, $200 per hour, and we were working on contingency. We made a demand for $100,000 and the attorney for Mr. Jones offered zero. Despite the fact that we had all of the evidence on our side and we stood an excellent chance of winning, the other attorney would not budge.

Prior to filing the lawsuit and over a period of several months, we kept talking but no progress was made. We were puzzled. Mr. Jones had a large and supposedly reputable company which handled investments for many entertainers and athletes. If we filed our suit the negative publicity would certainly injure Mr. Jones' business and reputation. Once we filed our suit, surely all the other investors would also sue. It did not make any business sense for Jones to attempt to defend his unwinnable position.

At last, we concluded that Jones simply did not grasp his legal position. We were sure that his attorneys were telling him that he had a great case and he should not settle. We figured that he had probably spent close to $35,000 in legal fees at this point. His attorneys were milking him and we were forbidden by the legal rules of ethics from speaking directly to Jones to let him know what was going on.

We finally decided that the only way to get through to Jones was to have an independent third party to talk some sense into him. We suggested to Jones' lawyer that we mediate the case with a well respected former judge. Each side would tell their story and the mediator would evaluate our claims. To our surprise he agreed.

Several weeks later we had our mediation. Attorneys for both sides were present along with our clients. We each informally presented our case and then the judge turned to Jones and said: "I have been a judge for many years and based on my experience I will tell you that if you go to trial you will lose. I don't know what your attorneys have been telling you but I suggest you settle this case right now."

Apparently this little speech did the trick. Within a week we had our client's $100,000 back plus interest of $30,000. That was more than we had asked for originally. Mr. Jones also paid about $65,000 in legal fees in addition to the settlement amount, so it ended up costing him $195,000 instead of the $100,000 we had been willing to take on day one.

This story is not uncommon. It is the rule. Every plaintiff's personal injury attorney who deals with insurance companies knows that once the case is in the hands of the insurance defense legal firm, no settlement will be possible until right before trial. Attorneys on an hourly fee basis will prolong the case for as long as possible

Expenses of Litigation

It is not just the attorney's fees that have to be calculated in determining whether to sue. The expenses of litigation must also be considered.

Everything connected with litigation seems to cost much more than it should. Fees to stenographers for a six hour deposition usually run $1,000 - $1,500. Nobody can figure out why it costs that much. When all of the costs of discovery, travel, expert witnesses, filing fees, research, private investigators and jury fees are added up the amount will be mind boggling. A normal range for expenses would be $15,000 to $75,000 in a case of modest complexity.

Contingent Fees

Contingent fee attorneys do not charge by the hour. Instead, their fee is a specified percentage of any recovery. This amount is usually 33 1/3% if the case is settled before trial and 40% if a trial is necessary. Since it is only large companies and very wealthy individuals who can afford to pay attorneys on an hourly bases for litigation, most lawsuits are handled on a contingent fee basis.

Usually the attorney agrees to advance all of the expenses and is repaid out of the recovery, if there is one. Although in most states the client is technically responsible for repaying expenses advanced by the attorney, it is rare that the attorney actually seeks to collect these amounts from his client. If there is no recovery, advances for costs are written off.

As opposed to hourly fee attorneys, who make money regardless of the outcome, the contingent fee attorney essentially bears all of the economic risk of the litigation. As we have seen, this risk and the potential reward can be quite substantial.

In this sense the contingent fee attorney is an entrepreneur. The attorney, rather then the client, must carefully evaluate the merits of a particular claim. The potential recovery is balanced against the amount of work which will be required. A fast settlement of marginal claims is essential to the plaintiff's lawyer. He simply cannot stay in business advancing costs and spending time on small cases.

On cases with potentially large damage awards, the plaintiff's attorney is willing to carry the case to trial. Usually he would prefer a fast settlement, but if he does not receive a satisfactory settlement offer he will go to trial. Many of these attorneys are really gamblers at heart and they are willing to invest a lot of time and money for a good size payoff. And in order to get this payoff, *the most important element of the case is finding a defendant who can pay.*

THE SEARCH FOR THE BIG BUCKS

Contingent fee attorneys love to have insurance companies, financial institutions or large businesses as the defendant. If he wins the attorney knows that he will collect, unless the amount of the judgment or the number of the claims causes the defendant to file for bankruptcy. That is what happened to A. H. Robbins (IUD) and Manville Corp. (asbestos). They each filed for bankruptcy to halt the flood of litigation over their products. But ordinarily, these type of companies make good defendants.

If a potential defendant is an individual or a small company, the plaintiff's attorney is going to do some very substantial investigation before he commits his time and his resources to the case. There is nothing that attorneys like less than working on a case without getting paid.

You must assume then, that the attorney interested in suing you will perform a very thorough financial investigation of your assets and income. This work will usually be done by one of the many private investigation firms that operate in each city.

The investigators will check the county records to locate any real estate which you own. In many counties these records are now computerized and available to the public so that this type of research is quite easy. This information reveals when the property was purchased, its value at that time, and the amount of any outstanding loans or other liens on the property.

Your credit history will be inspected. The information can be obtained from the credit reporting agencies. These reports contain a wealth of valuable material concerning your financial condition. Your payment history is revealed and quite possibly the name of your bank. The investigators then can get more detailed information about your banking records and accounts from their friendly sources in the bank. Even without inside sources, the investigator often poses as a potential lender or other authorized person, which will frequently cause your bank to divulge supposedly confidential information.

Some of the credit reporting agencies now offer a service where they ask you to fill out a financial statement, listing your assets and liabilities, which will be reported on your credit report. The agencies claim that this will make it convenient for your lender if you ever apply for a loan. In reality, they are merely making it easier for your creditors to find out what you own. Needless to say, *never provide the credit reporting agencies with your financial statement.*

If the name of your bank is not on the credit report and you have not previously given this information to the plaintiff, the investigators will resort to other strategies. One of these tricks is to send you a letter from a phony company with a check for five or ten dollars. The letter will say that the check is a refund from your long distance carrier or other utility. Most people receiving a check do not think about it too much. So, if you are like most people, you'll deposit the check in your bank account. When the canceled check is returned to the investigator, the endorsement on the back will reveal the name of your bank and your account number. With that information in hand, the investigator can discover your bank balance and monitor your account.

To find out whether you have any brokerage accounts, the investigator may call you, posing as a stockbroker soliciting business. The typical response is to say: "Sorry I already have an account somewhere else." The investigator will ask you where the account is and most likely you will tell him. It is amazing the things people will reveal to perfect strangers on the telephone.

These schemes are necessary because a plaintiff generally cannot obtain financial information directly from the defendant during the lawsuit. This information is usually not considered to be relevant to the underlying case, so the defendant cannot be compelled to answer questions about these matters. Unless the plaintiff's attorney has a good idea about the collectability of a judgment in the early stages of the case, he is not likely to proceed.

The financial investigation will produce one of three results:

- Substantial, relatively reachable assets are located. The decision will be made to file the lawsuit;

- Insufficient assets are located to provide a worthwhile recovery. The lawsuit will not be filed;

- No asset information is discovered one way or another. This is a rare occurrence but it happens.

Since the attorney cannot develop a level of confidence that sufficient assets exist to pay a judgment, in all likelihood the case will not be commenced.

If the attorney is acting on an hourly basis rather then a contingency, the issue of collectability is a problem for the client but not the lawyer, since the lawyer expects to get paid regardless of the outcome. In most cases, any mentally sound plaintiff will have his attorney perform a financial investigation of the defendant, prior to incurring substantial expenses in the case. If insufficient assets are discovered, only the most self-destructive of clients would elect to proceed with the case.

DEFENDANTS COSTS

If you are in the unfortunate position of being a defendant in a lawsuit, your lawyer will charge you on an hourly basis. No lawyers *defend* cases on a contingency arrangement. Like the lawyer representing the plaintiff on a time spent basis, you will be obligated to pay him whether you win or lose. What's more, your lawyer will undoubtedly require that you deposit a retainer to cover his anticipated expenses and costs as well. If you are a wealthy or seemingly wealthy person, your lawyer may tend to view you as a "meal ticket." And, come to think about it, *that is exactly what you are.*

Getting back to our example, the financial investigation of John Williams revealed that he owned a home with about $100,000 of equity, a savings account at a bank with $65,000, and a brokerage account with $135,000 of securities. The decision was made to file the lawsuit.

THE PLEADINGS STAGE

The Nightmare Begins

The initial pleading in a case is the "Complaint" which is prepared on behalf of the plaintiff and sets forth the allegations of the defendant's wrongdoing. The Complaint is filed in the appropriate local court and this filing commences the lawsuit.

In the usual case, the Complaint is produced by the plaintiff's attorney from one of a number of standard forms relating to the particular subject matter of the lawsuit. It is not necessary that the Complaint set forth anything other than the vaguest allegations of wrongdoing. The material facts are left to be uncovered during the Discovery process.

In our case, John Williams first learned that he was being sued when the Complaint was served on him by a process server. In reading it, Williams saw that he was being sued for defamation by the religious sect. It alleged that Williams willfully and maliciously printed false statements about the group and asked for actual damages of $100,000 and punitive damages of $5,000,000.

Of course, Williams was distraught. He had known that the leaders of the sect would be angry about the publication of his book, but because he had been truthful and accurate in his reporting, he had not felt there would be any grounds for a lawsuit. Now, he knew that, groundless or not, he would have to incur substantial expenses in defending the lawsuit and that a considerable amount of his resources and time would be consumed in the process.

A friend of Williams referred him to a local lawyer who agreed to represent him in the defense. The attorney informed Williams that he would have to file a response (or "Answer") to the Complaint within thirty days and after that, the Discovery phase of the lawsuit would begin. He advised Williams that the costs of the defense could not accurately be estimated but a good guess was somewhere between $25,000 and $75,000. Williams paid his attorney a $15,000 retainer fee. Within the proper time period, the Answer was filed denying each and every allegation.

Pre-Judgment Attachments

A powerful weapon in the hands of the plaintiff is the Pre-Judgment Writ of Attachment. This remedy is used to freeze the assets of the defendant and place them under court protection prior to a judgment. This procedure is designed to prevent the defendant from transferring, hiding or wasting his assets before the plaintiff has a chance to collect. Cash held in a savings or checking account cannot be reached by the defendant once a Pre-Judgment Writ of Attachment has been issued. Similarly, real estate cannot be sold or refinanced.

A Pre-Judgment Writ can be issued only in some types of cases. Usually, it is available only in contract cases arising from a commercial transaction. It is not available against a defendant in a negligence suit. The plaintiff's claim must be for a specific dollar amount and he must demonstrate a substantial likelihood that he will win at trial.

If a Pre-Judgment Writ is granted by the court, enumerated assets which are owned by the defendant are effectively frozen. As a result, the defendant may be unable to obtain working capital to carry on his business and unless he has a source of funds unknown to the plaintiff, the issuance of the Writ can force the defendant to accept a fast and unfavorable settlement.

In our example, the Plaintiff's claim against Williams did not arise out of a contract or a commercial transaction. The Writ was, therefore, not available for the Plaintiff.

DISCOVERY

Burying The Opposition

The Discovery phase of a lawsuit allows each side to probe the other side for facts as well as legal theories which might be helpful to build one's case and further elucidate the other side's trial strategy. Information is obtained from the opposing party by means of written questions (or "interrogatories"), face to face interrogation (or "oral depositions") and requests for the production of documents. This is the stage of a lawsuit where one party may attempt to "bury" the opponent in paper work. Typically, the side with the greatest financial resources now attempts to burden the other side to the greatest extent possible, in order to exhaust the opponents' financial resources. This can be accomplished by lengthy and numerous interrogatories, depositions and subpoenas of documents, all of which are designed to cause the opponent to incur needless legal fees, embarrassment, expenses and the greatest amount of overall aggravation

It is a customary tactic in Discovery to attempt to uncover those intimate and personal details about the defendant's life and habits that he would not wish to have revealed in a public trial. The objective of the opposing attorney is to gather as much "dirt" as possible, with the hope of increasing his bargaining position in the settlement negotiations prior to trial.

Often, medical and psychiatric evaluations are permitted, including blood and urine testing to search for evidence of drug use or illness. Lawyers are permitted extraordinary leeway in the ostensible search for items which may have even the most remote relevance to the underlying case.

Shortly after filing the Answer, Williams was served with over one hundred pages of interrogatories with questions concerning nearly every detail of his life. He was also required to submit to five days of depositions during which time he was questioned by the attorneys for the religious sect. All of the written notes which John had made in preparation for writing the book, including notes from his conversations with various confidential sources were subpoenaed and ordered to be turned over by the court. Many of Williams family and friends were also subjected to extensive interrogation on the dubious grounds that they possessed some information which might possibly be relevant to the case.

TRIAL

By the time the case was ready to go to trial, four years after the original Complaint was filed, he had paid his attorney $85,000 and his attorney estimated that the cost of the trial might exceed an additional $50,000. Williams attorney was approached by the Plaintiff's counsel, who offered to settle the case, if Williams would pay the religious sect $35,000. Since this amount was less than the cost of the trial and less than the amount that Williams stood to lose if there had been a judgment against him, Williams accepted the offer and settled the case for the amount proposed. By accepting this proposal, he managed to save his house and still had nearly $85,000 in his savings account. The religious sect had proposed the settlement, because they really did not wish to go to trial and possibly lose the case with the resulting negative publicity. Instead, they felt that they had accomplished their dual objective of punishing John and discouraging future journalistic attempts to reveal information about the sect.

Had Williams gone to trial and won, he would not have been entitled to recover his legal fees and costs. In the United States, each party to a lawsuit is required to pay his own costs and expenses. This is known as the "American Rule." In some other countries, such as England and Japan, the prevailing party is entitled to recover his attorney's fees. The exception to the American Rule is that parties to a contract may specify in the agreement that in the event of a dispute, the prevailing party is entitled to recover any costs incurred in a lawsuit, including legal fees. But unless that "attorney's fees" provision is included in a contract, each side bears its own expenses.

Concern about legal fees and costs are usually only one component in the defendant's willingness to settle a case before trial. A second and perhaps more compelling influence is that the outcome of a trial can never be predicted. No one knows which facts will be important and whose testimony will be believed. A sympathetic or attractive plaintiff or a skillful attorney will often sway the emotions of the jury despite a complete lack of merit to the case.

The ultimate amount of the damage award also cannot be predicted with any level of confidence. One of our clients, a successful business owner, told us that he had previously been sued by a former employee on a completely outrageous and frivolous claim. Prior to trial he turned down an offer to settle the case for $25,000, refusing to pay what he felt was pure "extortion" money. You can imagine his surprise when the jury awarded the plaintiff $750,000—based entirely on manufactured and per-jured testimony.

Unfortunately, it is clear to anyone who has ever been through the process that truth and justice count for very little in the courtroom. The most charitable interpretation is that the outcome of a particular case is determined purely by the random whim of a judge or jury. A more malevolent view is that judges and juries are often engaged in a form of wealth redistribution—taking from those who have it and giving it to those who don't.

COLLECTING YOUR ASSETS

The Wolf at Your Door

If Williams had lost the trial, the case would have then moved on to the collection stage of the lawsuit. Let's assume that there had been a judgment against Williams in the amount of $300,000. He could appeal the judgment to a higher court, but he would be required to post a security bond equal to the amount of judgment. He would obtain such a bond through a licensed bonding company that would require him to post security equal to the $300,000 bond. During the time that the case is on appeal, the judgment creditor would not be permitted to take any steps to collect on the judgment. After the appeals were exhausted (assuming Williams was able to pay for the costs of the appeals), the judgment creditor would then begin the collection process.

This process often begins with the procedure known as the debtor's examination. As stated, during the Discovery phase of the lawsuit, the plaintiff is generally prohibited from obtaining information concerning the defendant's assets. Typically, this information is not considered to be relevant to the underlying case and no discovery with regard to the defendant's assets is permitted.

After judgment, however, location of the debtor's assets becomes the focus of the investigation. The debtor's exam may be presented by written questions or by oral examination. In either case, the debtor will be asked to list and describe all of his assets and to provide all banking records. He will also be asked whether he has made any transfers of any property by gift prior to or during the pendency of the lawsuit. All of these questions are asked under oath and the failure to provide true and complete answers is a felony.

The procedure for enforcing judgments and collection by a judgment creditor is established by the laws of each state. For our example, we will assume that our debtor, John Williams, is a resident of California. Although each state has a different procedure, there is enough similarity in concept to provide you with a general understanding of the collection process.

Personal Property

When a judgment has been entered, the court issues a Writ of Execution which is essentially an authorization for the collection action. The judgment creditor gives the Writ of Execution to the marshall (or sheriff) with written instructions describing the property to be seized. The marshall is authorized to take possession of your property by removing it to a place of safe keeping or otherwise taking control over it. Property seized in this manner may then be sold at a public sale.

If your property is in the hands of a third party, the marshall directs that party to turn over the property. Your bank accounts and brokerage accounts can be seized in this manner. If a third party owes you money, that person is notified that he must make payment directly to the marshall's office.

Real Estate

The collection procedure for your real estate begins with the filing of a summary of the judgment ("Abstract of Judgment") with the County Recorder in each county where you own property. The Abstract of Judgment creates a lien on the property, similar to a mortgage or deed of trust. The creditor does not have to designate the address of the property or, for that matter, must he even know in advance that you own any real estate in that location. The lien applies to any real estate which you own in that county and also applies to any real estate which you purchase in the future.

Once this Abstract has been filed your property cannot be sold or refinanced without satisfying the judgment. You cannot avoid this lien by transferring the property to a third party. The lien remains attached to the property until the judgment is satisfied or expires. In California, judgment liens are in effect for ten years and can then be renewed for another ten years.

If the creditor does not want to wait for a voluntary sale or refinancing, he may file a Writ of Execution with the County Recorder. After giving proper notice to you, the property is then sold to the highest bidder at a public sale. Cash from the sale is applied to the amount of the judgment, including interest and expenses of collection. Any surplus is returned to you.

Real estate which is sold at these type of public auctions rarely brings in an amount greater than 50-

60% of the actual value of the property. As a result, if there is a $100,000 judgment against you, a creditor may seize and liquidate $200,000 of your property before the debt and the costs are satisfied. The judgment of $100,000 just cost you $200,000, not including your legal fees and costs.

Exempt and Partially Exempt Property

With an aim toward avoiding the complete impoverishment of a debtor, the law provides certain partial or complete exemptions from the sale of certain property by a creditor for the collection of his judgment. For purposes of illustration, the following is an *incomplete* list of exempt property under California law:

Government Benefits

Unemployment benefits, disability and health payments and benefits under the Workers Compensation law are exempt from collection.

Life Insurance

State laws vary considerably on whether any or all of the cash value of insurance policies is subject to collection by a creditor. California exempts up to $4,000 in cash value as well as life insurance proceeds which are reasonably necessary for the support of the debtor's family. In Texas and Pennsylvania, insurance annuities are entirely exempt.

Wages

Each state provides for a different degree of exemption of wages from garnishment. Garnishment is the procedure whereby a debtor's employer is directed to withhold some portion of the debtor's salary. The amount withheld is then turned over directly to the creditor. In California, up to 75% of the debtors disposable earnings are exempt from garnishment.

Household Furnishings and Automobiles

In California, the debtor may exempt ordinary and necessary household furnishings, apparel, appliances, and other personal effects at the debtor's residence. Items having extraordinary value, such as antiques, musical instruments or art work, are subject to execution. The debtor is entitled to proceeds from the sale of these items in an amount necessary to purchase a replacement of ordinary value. Automobiles for personal use are exempt up to $1,200.

Personal Residences

The personal residence of a debtor may be partially protected by the filing of a Homestead Exemption for a dwelling in which the debtor resides. In California, the amount of the exemption ranges from $50,000 to $100,000 depending upon whether family members are living at the residence and whether the debtor is over 65 years of age.

Some states have particularly liberal Homestead Exemptions. Florida allows a Homestead of 1/2 acre for urban property and 160 acres for property in rural areas. Texas provides protection for one acre of urban land and up to 200 acres for rural property. In Massachusetts, the exemption is $100,000 for a family residence and $150,000 for a disabled individual over age of 65.

Retirement Plans

IRA and Keogh plans are granted an exemption to the extent of reasonable retirement needs. Corporate pension and profit sharing plans, formed under ERISA, are fully exempt from judgment creditors.

Business Property

Property used in the business or profession in which the debtor earns his living is exempt in California to the extent of $2,500 of equity. The exemption applies to tools, books, equipment, one commercial vehicle and other personal property.

Interests in Trusts

Under the law in California and many other states, where a trust provides that a beneficiary's interest cannot be transferred, the interest is exempt from execution, until the amount is actually paid to the beneficiary. Also, if a trust requires the trustee to pay income or principal for the support or education of a beneficiary, these amounts are not reachable, until paid.

If a debtor sets up a trust in which he is a beneficiary, the law in California allows a creditor to reach everything in the trust. In Chapter Seven we will look at how some kinds of trusts can be used to protect personal assets. But a trust in which the debtor is also a beneficiary will not be useful for this purpose.

HOW TO DEFEND YOURSELF

CHAPTER 4

CREATING THE ASSET PROTECTION PLAN

At this point we have seen that almost everyone faces a real risk of getting sued. A lawsuit will be exceedingly expensive and time consuming to defend and if you lose, the judgment creditor has broad powers to seize almost everything you own.

The objectives of an asset protection plan are to discourage potential lawsuits before they begin by minimizing your risk of personal liability and holding your property in a protected form which will take away the economic incentive for someone to sue you. As we have discussed, in this context, it is extremely unlikely that anyone would wish to sue you—or that any attorney would be willing to accept a case against you—if your assets were safely insulated and shielded against this type of attack.

PLAYING SMART DEFENSE

Use a Corporation to Do Business

One of the best ways to keep from being sued personally is to avoid conducting business in your own name. You can do this by interposing a legal entity between yourself and the rest of the world. This entity would be responsible for all business activities. Purchases and sales, contracts, loans, leases, and other obligations would be executed solely in the name of the entity.

Typically, a corporation is used for these purposes. A corporation is an organization with a separate and distinct legal existence. Shareholders, officers and directors are not personally liable for debts incurred by a corporation. Corporations are sanctioned by the law of every state, precisely for the purpose of allowing individuals to conduct business in a form which will legally limit their potential liability.

A corporation must be differentiated from a sole proprietorship and a partnership. When a person conducts business as a sole proprietor, he is personally liable for all obligations of the business. The same is true with a partnership. Each partner has personal liability for the debts of the partnership.

The owner of a corporation, on the other hand, is not liable for its debts. Obligations of a corporation are not the responsibility of the owner, unless the owner specifically agrees to be responsible for that debt.

Businesses which are particularly amenable to the corporate form are those which involve the purchase and sale of goods. Manufacturers, wholesalers, and retailers will find that conducting business as a corporation will effectively insulate the owners from many types of potential liability. Those people who are in service type businesses will enjoy protection from some but not all forms of liability. These issues will be discussed in greater detail in Chapter Six. For now, it's important to note that advantage should be taken of every legal means of limiting potential liability and using a corporation to conduct business will generally be an important first step in achieving this objective.

Avoid Joint Relationships

You can also reduce your exposure to lawsuits by avoiding, whenever possible, some of the sources of potential liability. One of the most significant of these sources is the joint and several liability associated with business partnerships.

As previously discussed, each partner is liable for any debts incurred by another partner on behalf of the business. Each partner is also liable for any negligent acts committed by another partner. Worst of all, however, joint and several liability means that a partner is not just responsible for his share of the obligation. Instead, each partner is responsible for the entire amount. If your partner cannot or will not pay his share, you pay the whole amount.

We can not emphasize strongly enough that these type of business arrangements must be avoided. Operating a business in partnership form is the single greatest threat to your financial well-being.

Over and over again in our practice we see this story. Mr. Wilson and Mr. Stevens each put in some money and form a partnership to carry on a business. Wilson and Stevens borrow money from the bank and sign a long-term lease for rental space. Some time later, during an economic downturn, business slows down. Cash flow becomes very tight. Wilson contributes additional funds to the partnership in order to meet expenses but Stevens does not have any savings and cannot contribute his share. Business continues to get worse and Stevens decides to file personal bankruptcy in order to be relieved of his obligations for the bank loan and the lease. At this point, Wilson is now solely responsible for the entire amount owed to the bank and the entire amount owed on the lease. Partnerships like this are the surest and fastest way to wipe out everything you own.

The only way to go into business with someone else is to do so using a corporate form or a limited liability company which is described in Appendix A. Using these arrangements, you will not be personally responsible for the debts of the company or the negligent acts of your co-owner. If a lender or a landlord requires your personal guarantee of an obligation, guarantee only your proportionate interest. If you are a 50% co-owner of the business, you can agree to guarantee only 50% of the debt. If the lender or landlord won't accept this arrangement, do not do the deal unless you are fully prepared to pay the entire amount.

Do Not Involve Your Spouse In Your Business

Another way to limit personal exposure to lawsuits is to remove your spouse from your business affairs. What we mean by this is that you should take precautions to insulate your spouse from any potential lawsuit liability.

One way to do this is to make sure that your spouse is not an officer or director of the corporation which you use for business. Many people believe they are demonstrating trust or love by making their spouse an officer or director. Almost every time a client comes to us with an existing corporation, we find that the spouse is listed as vice-president or secretary of the company. This is a mistake.

If there is a lawsuit against the corporation, all of the officers and directors will typically be named as defendants. We will discuss later the potential liability of officers and directors, but for now, regardless of whether the suit will be successful, you certainly want to avoid exposing the assets of a spouse to potential liability.

In a similar vein, you should not allow a spouse to co-sign on loans, leases or other obligations. Often, a lender or landlord will ask you to get your spouse's signature on a contract. This is usually not a condition of the deal but is more a matter of course.

We suggest that you politely refuse any such request. You can explain that your spouse is not involved in your business affairs and it is your policy not to provide her signature. That should work and if it doesn't, take your business someplace else. You do not want your spouse to incur a potential liability and subject his or her assets to the risks of the particular venture.

ASSET PROTECTION GAME PLAN

The steps suggested so far will be helpful in protecting assets from lawsuit liability, because the exposure to lawsuits will be reduced. But the best way to discourage lawsuits is to protect your assets from the claims of a potential creditor. If someone is thinking about suing you, they will investigate your financial resources. If they are unable to locate any assets which are available to satisfy a judgment, they will probably not proceed. Even if the plaintiff still wants to go forward, no contingent fee attorney will accept a case against a "judgment proof" defendant. Creating an asset protection plan will knock out almost any lawsuit before it begins. And if somebody does go ahead with the suit, the goal is to make sure they cannot collect anything if they win.

Asset protection planning requires an understanding of a variety of legal devices and strategies. When we create an asset protection plan, a combination of techniques involving corporations, gifts, trusts and limited partnerships is used. In this section, we will provide a brief overview of the basic strategies and, in subsequent Chapters, we will discuss each of the elements in greater detail.

Family Limited Partnerships

In general, an asset protection plan involves the use of a device known as a *limited partnership*. A limited partnership is a particular form of a partnership which has one or more general partners who are responsible for management and control of partnership affairs. A general partner has unlimited liability for the obligations of the partnership. There is also one or more limited partners in the partnership. Limited partners have no say in the activities of the partnership. Their role is strictly passive and they have no liability for any partnership obligations.

In order to insulate family assets from potential lawsuit liability, we create a limited partnership which we will refer to as a Family Limited Partnership (FLP). Usually, Husband and Wife will be the general partners of the FLP. We will then transfer into the

FLP all of the valuable family assets, including the house, other real estate, savings accounts and business interests. When we have a client who is single, he will serve as the sole general partner. We will then bring in a friend or family member, or a new legal entity to hold a small fractional interest in the FLP.

The reason for the FLP arrangement is that the law of each state provides that *a creditor of a partner cannot reach inside the partnership to seize partnership assets.* Partnership assets are protected from execution for the debts of one of the partners. A creditor of one of the partners has no claim against the property belonging to the partnership.

What then does the creditor get? The only thing that a creditor can reach is any distributions made by the partnership to the debtor partner. That means amounts which are actually paid out of the partnership to the debtor must be turned over to the creditor to the extent of the judgment. *If the partnership does not make any distributions to the debtor, there is nothing for the creditor to take.*

Applying these principles to the FLP arrangement, we can see that the law provides an excellent vehicle for asset protection. Let's look at the possibilities in a little more detail.

Assume that Husband owns a business with a high risk of lawsuits. Wife is a principal at a local elementary school and probably has a low level of exposure. All family assets are transferred into a FLP.

Husband and Wife are each general partners, thereby retaining co-equal management and control over the family wealth. As general partners, Husband

and Wife could have an ownership interest of only one or two percent. In order to control the partnership, it is not necessary to own a majority of the partnership interests. This is different than with a corporation. The shareholders of a corporation elect a board of directors who control the affairs of the corporation. The rule is usually one share - one vote. A majority shareholder thereby has absolute control over a corporation. In a limited partnership the limited partners cannot vote on most matters and cannot vote to remove the general partners (unless the partnership agreement gives them that right). Control of a limited partnership is solely in the hands of the general partners, no matter what percentage they own.

Asset Protection Plan #1

Because Husband can maintain control over the assets of the partnership without owning any significant percentage of partnership interests, a variety of different techniques can be used, depending upon the particular circumstances. For instance, if he chooses, Husband can hold a 1% interest as general partner and a 49% interest as a limited partner. Wife would own exactly the same percentages. This set up is illustrated in Figure 4-1.

Under this arrangement, if Husband were to be successfully sued, the judgment creditor would have the right to take any distributions from the partnership to the Husband. This may or may not be troublesome. If the assets of the partnership do not generate income and the Husband cannot foresee circumstances where he would need to liquidate and distribute partnership assets, this type of arrangement may work very well. For example, if assets consist primarily of a house and stock of a family business, the partnership would not be generating any cash flow for distribution to the partners. A judgment creditor with the right to seize any distributions on Husband's 50% partnership interest would receive nothing, until a partnership distribution is made to Husband.

Asset Protection Plan #2

A second alternative would also have Husband and Wife as general partners, each with a 1% interest. But instead of Husband owning a 49% limited partnership interest, Wife would own all of these interests. Husband would be a 1% general partner with Wife and she would own the remaining 98% as a limited partner. This arrangement essentially involves a gift of Husband's interest in family assets from Husband to Wife. This is illustrated in Figure 4-2.

This set-up would be useful if family assets consisted of income producing investments and the income was necessary for the support of the family. Suppose the principle asset was an investment account worth $500,000, generating $40,000 per year in income. Since the family needs these funds to pay expenses, it would not be convenient to withhold distributions if a judgment creditor was present. Now, however, since Husband owns only a 1% interest, a creditor would have a right to only 1% of the distributions. Wife, who owns a 99% interest, could take 99% of the partnership income free of the creditors claim. This income could be used to provide support for the family.

Asset Protection Plan #3

A third arrangement involves the use of an irrevocable trust created for the benefit of children or grandchildren. Husband and Wife still own 1% each as general partners. The trust would own the other 98%. (See Figure 4-3). This set-up is used when Wife is equally vulnerable to lawsuits or when partnership assets generate income which is not necessary for the support of the family. Under this arrangement, a creditor of Husband or Wife would have no right to the income distributed to the trust. The trust could accumulate income or provide for distributions in the discretion of the trustee. Husband and Wife could be the trustees of the trust.

Asset Protection Plan #4

A fourth alternative is to transfer a 98% limited partnership interest into an Asset Protection Trust, established in a favorable offshore jurisdiction. (See Figure 4-4). For reasons which we will explore, these types of trusts are usually the most powerful vehicles used in the asset protection field. These arrangements provide the highest degree of control and flexibility and will generally accomplish the objectives which Husband and Wife desire. The use of these trusts will be discussed in greater detail in Chapter Nine.

Each of these arrangements involves legal, tax and business considerations, all of which must be properly understood in order to create an asset protection plan, which will be suitable for you. In the subsequent Chapters, after looking at the legal re-

strictions on these arrangements, we will discuss corporations, gifts, trusts, and partnerships. We will see
how they work together in developing effective strategies for asset protection.

HOW TO DEFEND YOURSELF

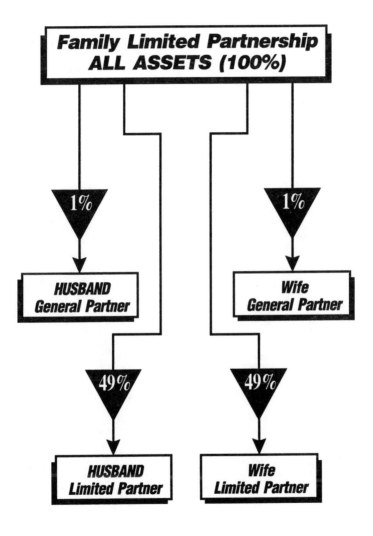

Figure 4-1

HOW TO DEFEND YOURSELF

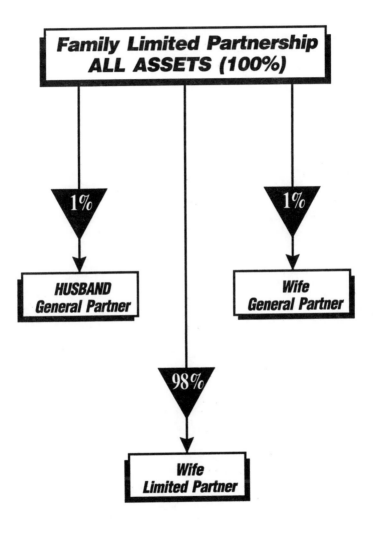

Figure 4-2

HOW TO DEFEND YOURSELF

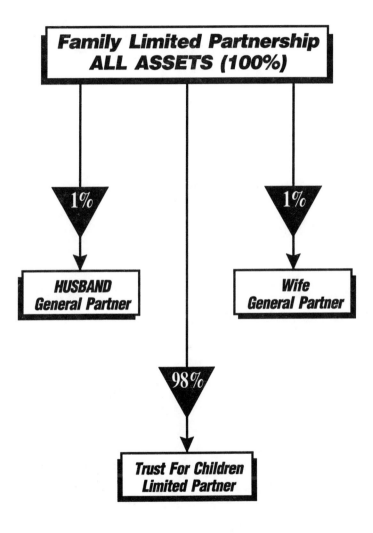

Figure 4-3

HOW TO DEFEND YOURSELF

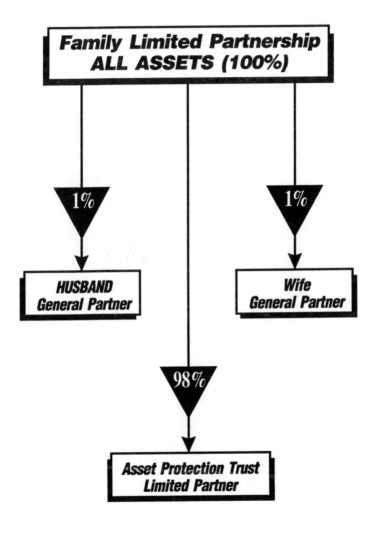

Figure 4-4

HOW TO AVOID FRAUDULENT TRANSFERS

Before creating any asset protection plan, it is necessary to understand the legal restrictions on transfers which impair the rights of a creditor.

For as long as there have been commercial transactions, people have attempted to conceal their ownership of property in order to defeat the claims of their creditors. Concealment may take the form of physically hiding money or jewelry, or it may take the form of "gifts" to friendly parties or relatives. Usually, such "gifts" are accompanied by secret agreements to return the property after the trouble has passed.

In an effort to protect creditors from this endless game of hide and seek, English speaking courts have, for approximately 400 years, sought to invalidate transfers made by a person with the intent to defraud his creditors. Any transfer of property which is proved to be a "fraudulent conveyance" may be set aside by a court. Under these circumstances, the transfer will be ignored and the property will be treated as if still owned by the debtor. That means that the property will then be available to be seized by the judgment creditor. This law is currently embodied in the Uniform Fraudulent Conveyance Act and the Uniform Fraudulent Transfer Act, which are similar in coverage and either of which is in effect in most states. For simplicity's sake, we will cover the California version which will, of course, vary in some respects from that of other states.

WHEN A TRANSFER IS FRAUDULENT

A transfer is subject to being set aside as a "fraudulent conveyance" in at least four circumstances:

- The transfer is made with the "actual intent to hinder, delay, or defraud any creditor of the debtor"

- The transfer does not involve the receipt of "reasonably equivalent value" *and* the person making the transfer becomes insolvent (or was insolvent prior to the exchange)

- The transfer does not include the receipt of "reasonably equivalent value" *and* the person making the transfer knows (or should have known) that with his remaining resources he will be unable to pay future debts; and/or

- The transfer is without "reasonably equivalent value" *and* the person making the transfer continues to operate a business with assets that are "unreasonably small" in relation to typical existing or proposed business transactions

A "transfer" encompasses not only the disposition of assets but taking on additional debt or obligations without receiving an equivalent benefit. For example, giving a friend a mortgage on your home without receiving the cash loan proceeds could qualify as a fraudulent transfer.

Actual Intent to Defraud

First let's examine the circumstances under which the "actual intent to defraud" exists. Since "intent" is a state of mind, which is not easy for a creditor to prove, courts have inferred from the facts and circumstances of each particular case whether the intent to defraud existed in the mind of a debtor. Those particular facts and circumstances have been branded the "badges of fraud," meaning their presence is consistent with an actual intent to defraud. The existence of two or more of these factors would allow a judge or jury to conclude that the purpose of the transfer was to unlawfully escape the payment of debts.

Badges of Fraud

Court cases involving the "badges of fraud" are numerous. Here is a *partial* list:

- The transfer of assets to a family member or a close friend

- The creation of a debt owed to a family member or a close friend

- The concealment or non-disclosure of the fact that a transfer has occurred or a debt was incurred

- A transfer occurring immediately before the transferor was sued or threatened with a suit

- The disappearance of the transferor

- The removal of assets

- The transferor's receipt of less than the true worth of the asset

- A transfer occurring shortly before or after a substantial debt was incurred; and

- A transfer of assets to another creditor who then transfers the same assets to a person friendly to the original transferor

DEFENSES TO FRAUDULENT CONVEYANCES

Conversely, a court or jury may take into account facts and circumstances that may imply that the purpose of the transfer was other than avoiding the payment of one's debts. Presumably, transfers associated with or made for legitimate business purposes would fit in this category as would transfers made for estate planning reasons. This creates an interesting paradox: on the one hand, transfers to a spouse or one's children have traditionally been looked upon suspiciously. However, since such transfers are common for accomplishing legitimate estate planning objectives, transfers and gifts which are consistent with valid estate planning motivation may be viewed as lacking the requisite intent to defraud a creditor. Similarly, a transfer to a corporation or other entity composed of one's spouse and children can have a legitimate estate planning or business motivation, or it may be accomplished purely as a way to avoid or reduce one's ability to pay debts.

In order to solve this dilemma, as early as 1601, courts have ruled that a good faith transfer to a trust, although providing substantial obstacles to a creditor's collection, could not be inferred to be fraudulent unless other "badges of fraud" also exist. In other words, the courts have tended to presume transfers to relatives, either directly or through other entities, are done without actual fraud unless some *other* circumstance is present so as to create the cumulative effect that the intent to defraud was involved.

Although cases on the topic do not provide much guidance, certain general principles of law can be drawn:

- The mere existence of the transfer without other suspicious activities is generally insufficient to establish fraudulent intent

- All of the facts and circumstances of the case and the credibility of the debtor-transferor are crucial in determining whether fraudulent intent exists; and

- Business or familial motivation for the transfer is critical in rebutting an inference that the transfer was accomplished primarily with the intent to avoid the payment of creditors

Statute of Limitations

An action by a creditor to set-aside a transfer as a fraudulent conveyance must be filed within a specified time period. For the creditor who is trying to prove an actual intent to defraud, the lawsuit must be filed on or before four years after the transfer was made or within one year from the date the transfer could have been reasonably discovered, whichever is later. In no event, however, can the lawsuit be started seven years after the date of transfer. In cases in which actual intent to defraud did not exist but "reasonably equivalent value" was not exchanged or a transfer rendered the debtor insolvent, the creditor must bring his suit within four years from the date the property was transferred.

FRAUDULENT CONVEYANCES AND ASSET PROTECTION

The ideal time to create an asset protection plan is before there are any potential creditors. That way, transfers to the Family Limited Partnership or to a trust should not fall within the fraudulent conveyance statutes.

If you make transfers at a time when a lawsuit is imminent or pending or at a time when you have an outstanding obligation, the outcome will be less certain. The success of the plan will be dependent upon your ability to demonstrate remaining solvency and a purpose for the arrangement other than an intent to defraud a creditor.

For instance, the Family Limited Partnership arrangement provides excellent estate planning benefits which will be discussed in the succeeding Chapters. When used in conjunction with an Asset Protection Trust, the overall structure provides a way to avoid the costs and expense of probate; a means of reducing estate taxes through a program of gifts; and a means of shifting income to lower tax bracket family members. Since all of these are worthwhile and valuable objectives, it may be extremely difficult for a creditor to establish that an intent to defraud was the motivation for creating the overall plan. This is particularly so if this plan is structured so that it cannot be claimed that you were rendered insolvent at the time the plan was established.

Ultimately the best defense will be to carefully document, with your attorney, the legitimate business and estate planning purposes of the arrangement. That will go a long way in countering a potential claim that the motivation involved a prohibited intent.

WHEN TO USE A CORPORATION

BUILDING THE FIRST LINE OF DEFENSE

A corporation will usually be an important component of any asset protection plan. If you engage in any business activities, those activities must be kept separate from the Family Limited Partnership. Since business activities carry a high potential for lawsuits, you will want to isolate and remove those activities from the entity where the family assets are kept. In this Chapter we will examine how a corporation fits in with the overall strategy.

Corporations are a form of business organization permitted by law in every state. A unique feature of a corporation is that it issues shares of stock. A share of stock entitles a shareholder to vote on the election of a board of directors who are charged with the overall management of the corporation. The board of directors elects the officers; the president, secretary and treasurer, who are authorized to conduct the day to day business. Many states permit a single individual to serve as sole director and to hold all of the corporate offices.

One of the singular features of a corporation is that it is intended to have a perpetual existence. The death of an individual director or officer does not terminate the existence of the corporation. Instead, the corporation carries on indefinitely until it is dissolved by a vote of the shareholders.

A corporation is legally formed and begins its existence upon the filing of Articles of Incorporation with the Secretary of State of the state of incorporation. You can choose to incorporate in any state you wish. It is not necessary to incorporate in the state where your business is located.

A disproportionately large number of corporations are formed in Delaware. Most large public companies are incorporated there. Delaware has encouraged corporate formations by adopting laws which favor incumbent officers and directors against attack from dissident shareholders. It also has a long history of decided court cases interpreting its corporate law and it has no state income tax. These are attractive features to consider when choosing a state for incorporating. Nevada is another state without corporate income tax and its laws are also designed to actively encourage new corporations.

LIMITING PERSONAL LIABILITY

The primary distinguishing feature of a corporation is the so called *limited liability* of the officers, directors and shareholders (the "principals") of the company. In a properly organized and maintained and capitalized corporation, the principals have no personal liability for debts of the corporation. If a corporation breaches an obligation or causes injury to a third party, only the corporation and not the principals are legally responsible. If the corporation does not have sufficient assets to satisfy the liability, the creditor is not entitled to seek satisfaction from the personal assets of the principals. This feature is distinct from other businesses operated as sole proprietorships, partnerships or trusts. In those cases, the owner, partner or trustee, respectively, has *unlimited liability* for debts incurred in the business.

Effect of Personal Guarantees

Anyone doing business with a corporation may require that the principal of the company give a personal guarantee of a corporate obligation. In simple terms, the person signing such a guarantee promises to pay the corporation's debts if the corporation is unable to do so. For example, if you wish to lease office or retail space for the business, the landlord may request a personal guarantee of the lease obligation. If the corporation fails to make its payments on time, the landlord can then collect directly from you. In this manner, a personal guarantee eliminates the benefits of the corporation's limited liability.

Similarly, vendors sometimes will not sell, and banks and other lenders often will not lend to a family corporation without a personal guarantee. To the extent that guarantees are provided, an individual owner will have personal liability for these contracts, and the corporation will not provide protection from these obligations.

Protection from Tort Claims

When the source of the lawsuit is a negligence claim or a claim arising out of the employer-employee relationship, the corporation will be a particularly effective device. We have previously discussed how an employee's negligence may be imputed to his employer. If your secretary injures someone while she is picking up your lunch, you are likely to be responsible for the damages. However, if the secretary is an employee of a corporation, the corporation, but not the officers or directors, will be liable for the injury. This is also the case for employee claims of discrimination or wrongful termination. Any such lawsuits will be filed against the corporation as the employer. The principals of the company will not usually be held personally liable for these type of activities.

Protection from Customers

When the corporation *sells* goods or services, liability for these activities will usually be limited to the corporation. A buyer of goods (as opposed to a seller) typically does not require a personal guarantee as to the quality of the product. If the product is faulty or someone is injured by the product, the corporation will be liable but not the principals. If a corporation supplies services, such as contracting or repair work on a house, only the corporation would be liable for faulty services. A corporation provides a very useful shield against personal liability in connection with the sale of products or services. When a corporation *buys* goods or services, liability for payment will also be limited to the corporation, unless the principals have signed a personal guarantee of the obligation.

HOW TO AVOID THE CORPORATE TAX

The Double Tax Problem

The way corporations are taxed provides some interesting and challenging planning decisions. A corporation is a taxpaying entity. That is, it must file an annual tax return and pay taxes on its income. If those earnings are distributed to a shareholder, this distribution is treated as a *dividend* which is then taxable to the shareholder. The effect of this is that corporate earnings are taxed twice—once at the corporate level and once at the shareholder level, when the earnings are distributed in the form of dividends.

The problem of double taxation may be eliminated in one of two ways. First, the corporation can pay out as salary an amount equal to its net earnings. This is called *zeroing out* the corporation. As an example, a family owned corporation in the construction business might have a profit of $100,000. If this amount is paid to one or more of the officers of the corporation as compensation for services, the corporation will get a tax deduction for this $100,000 in salary. That will reduce taxable income to zero and no federal income taxes would be due. The $100,000 is included in income and the tax is paid by the recipient. This eliminates the problem of double taxation.

The Internal Revenue Code imposes certain limitations on this technique by allowing a deduction to the corporation, only if the amount of compensation paid to a particular individual is "reasonable." The salary cannot be excessive based upon the actual services provided by the individual. There have been literally thousands of cases litigated by the IRS on this issue and no firm rule has developed. Basically, if the salary is comparable to that received by others in similar businesses, it is unlikely that there will be a challenge from the IRS.

If you attempt to pay salary to your children or your grandmother without any services performed by them, the deduction could be disallowed as unreasonable. If the salary is disallowed as unreasonable, this amount is added back to the corporation's income and a tax is assessed on this income. Also, the amount which was distributed is treated as a dividend to the recipient and is taxable to that individual. This produces a double tax on the same income and is clearly a disastrous result.

Using S Corporations

The second method for eliminating double taxation is the use of a device called an *S Corporation* This is a type of corporation specifically provided for in the Internal Revenue Code. An S Corporation is treated differently for tax purposes then a conventional corporation (which is known as a "C Corporation"). If elected by the shareholders, an S Corporation will not be subject to tax at the corporate level. Instead, all corporate income is included directly in the income of the shareholders. There is no need to zero out the corporation with salaries since corporate income is now subject to tax only once, at the shareholder level. Additionally, if the corporation has a *net loss*, that loss can be used by

WHEN TO USE A CORPORATION

the shareholders to offset other business income. In order to qualify, the stock of an S Corporation must be held by 35 or fewer individuals and all shareholders must consent to the election. An S Corporation has all of the lawsuit protection features of a C Corporation. If unreasonable compensation is an issue or the corporation is expected to show net losses, an S Corporation would be a useful planning technique.

PIERCING THE CORPORATE VEIL

The lawsuit protection features of the corporation will be available only if the integrity of the corporation as a separate and distinct entity, apart from the individual, is respected by a court and by the Internal Revenue Service. In matters involving a lawsuit by an injured party, especially if a corporation has no significant assets, the plaintiff will attempt to convince the court that the corporate entity should not be respected and that the principals of the company should be personally liable. In these cases, the plaintiff is attempting to *pierce the corporate veil* in order to obtain a judgment against the principals, who may have personal assets sufficient to satisfy a judgment.

There are many reported cases on this topic and the outcome is usually determined by whether the corporation carries out its business and looks and acts the way a corporation should. If the principals treat the corporation and hold out the corporation to third parties as a separate and distinct entity, the court will uphold the status of the corporation and will not find personal liability. However, if various corporate formalities are not consistently observed, the corporation will be disregarded and the individuals may be held personally liable.

The corporate formalities which the courts have determined to be of particular significance are as follows:

Corporate Bylaws

The corporation must adopt a set of Bylaws, which provide a written statement of how the internal affairs of the corporation will be handled. The Bylaws set the time and place of regular shareholder meetings and meetings of the board of directors.

Corporate Minute Book

The corporate minute book contains a written record of actions by the shareholders and directors of the corporation. At a minimum, there must be annual minutes reflecting the election of directors by the shareholders. Any significant corporate activities, including corporate borrowings, purchases and the payment of compensation to officers, should be properly reflected in the minutes of the meetings of the directors and shareholders.

Stock Ledger Book

The corporation must maintain an accurate stock ledger book. This is the book which shows who has been issued stock certificates and the amounts received by the corporation for the issuance of its stock. The stock ledger book contains an up to date record of the names and number of shares owned by each shareholder.

Conducting Business in Corporate Name

When doing business with third parties, the officers and directors must make it clear that they are acting on behalf of the corporation and not in their individual capacity. Correspondence should be sent out under the proper corporate letterhead and contracts should be entered into only with the corporation as a signatory. Unless the documents clearly reflect that a transaction is entered into on behalf of the corporation and all necessary agreements are entered into under the corporation's name, the corporate entity will not survive a challenge in a lawsuit.

Bank Accounts

Corporate bank accounts and accounting records must be separate and distinct from the individual. A corporate bank account cannot be treated as if it were the account of the individual officer or director. Corporate income and assets must be separately accounted for on the books of the corporation. One of the biggest mistakes made by clients is that they feel free to move money and property back and forth between themselves and their corporation without properly accounting for such movement in the records of the corporation. This is a fatal mistake and under these circumstances the corporate entity will be disregarded by the court.

PROTECTING CORPORATE ASSETS

As discussed, conducting your business as a corporation provides numerous asset protection benefits. If the corporate formalities are followed, you will not be liable for corporate obligations, except those which you have personally guaranteed. This is a very significant protection. If your corporation conducts an active business, buying and selling goods or providing services, lawsuits arising out of these dealings will involve only the corporation. Your personal assets will not be at risk in these transactions.

But what happens if the corporation gets sued? We know that because of its active business dealings, there is a high likelihood that the corporation will get sued at some point. What will happen to corporate assets if it loses the lawsuit?

The corporation's assets are at risk just like yours are. If the corporation loses a lawsuit, all of its assets are available for collection. Because of this, a sensible asset protection strategy must be adopted for the corporation as well as for the individual.

As a rule to the extent practical, you do not want the corporation to hold any significant assets. You do not want a corporation to build up a substantial net worth only to see everything wiped out in the event of a lawsuit.

Real Estate and Equipment

Assets, such as real estate and equipment, should never be held by the corporation. These assets should be held in the Family Limited Partnership and leased back to the corporation at a reasonable rent. Since the property will be leased, rather than owned, the assets will not be available for collection by a creditor of the corporation.

Surplus Cash

The corporation should never hold any surplus cash. You would be amazed at how often clients proudly tell us that they have accumulated $1,000,000 of cash in a Merrill-Lynch CMA account. This is pure madness. Only amounts necessary to pay immediate and foreseeable obligations should remain in the corporate account. Any surplus should be loaned or paid out as salary or some other type of distribution. The last thing you want is a fat pile of cash sitting around waiting for a creditor.

Inventory and Accounts Receivable

Certain types of property can't be conveniently held outside of the corporation. Assets, such as inventory and accounts receivable, will undoubtedly cause tax and accounting difficulties, unless they are maintained in corporate form.

If these types of assets are significant in value, one solution is to create liens which will have priority over subsequent creditors. For example, the owners of the business can make loans to the corporation for working capital or other needs. As security for these advances, the corporation can give the owners, as collateral, a lien on corporate inventory and receivables. This security interest is called a UCC-1 filing under the provisions of the Uniform Commercial Code. The hoped for result of this UCC-1 filing is that the inventory and receivables will be protected. A judgment creditor would find that the equity in these assets is subject to the superior claim of the business owners and cannot be used to satisfy the judgment.

Multiple Corporations

If the business of the corporation can be divided into separate businesses, assets can be protected through the use of multiple corporations. For example, a single corporation may own and operate six retail stores in different locations. If something happens at one of the stores, giving rise to potential liability, the assets of the other successful stores must be isolated from these claims.

A client of ours had four fast food restaurants in different locations. All of the stores were held in one corporation. Business at one of the locations slowed down substantially. That store became a financial drain on the others, absorbing all of the available cash in the company. Eventually, the corporation had to file for bankruptcy, wiping out all of the equity that had been built up.

Our approach would have been to have each restaurant separately incorporated. Then, if one business were to falter, it would not drag down the others. A judgment creditor of one corporation would not be able to reach the assets of the other companies. An extreme illustration of this is the taxi-cab company which separately incorporated twenty six different taxis.

This strategy is also useful for a company which manufactures or wholesales different product lines. Companies in the pharmaceutical business face enormous potential liability for many types of drugs and medical devices. Witness the bankruptcy of A. H. Robbins caused by liability in connection with the IUD's it produced. Dow Corning has had similar problems from the silicone breast implants it has been selling. Whenever a particular product may be hazardous, using multiple corporations is an effective technique for insulating each separate product from liability caused by another.

The stock of each corporation can be held by the individual owner or by a corporate holding company. These two arrangements are illustrated in Figures 6-1 and 6-2. For asset protection purposes the shares in either example can be held by the Family Limited Partnership. This is illustrated in Figure 6-3.

USING CORPORATIONS TO PROTECT PERSONAL ASSETS

The question often asked is whether a corporation can be used to shield a shareholder's personal assets from his creditors. The answer is that a corporation can be used for this purpose under certain circumstances.

A judgment creditor of an individual can levy upon any shares of stock owned by that person. If a person transfers assets to a corporation in exchange for stock, the creditor simply levies upon the stock certificates and becomes the owner of those shares. If he obtains over 50% of the shares, the creditor is then in control of the company—and your assets. This result differs from the Family Limited Partnership arrangement where the creditor cannot get voting control over the partnership and therefore cannot reach the assets held by the partnership. Since the shares of stock of a corporation are reachable by judgment creditors, a corporation will not provide a significant degree of asset protection for an individual who owns those shares, in the event of a successful lawsuit against him.

Asset protection can be accomplished if the owner moves the shares into a protected position. If Wife is less vulnerable to a lawsuit then Husband, share ownership could be transferred to her. However, since Wife would then have full voting control over the corporation, this would leave Husband in a dangerous position. Husband could not be assured of continuous or co-equal management of the corporation in the event of a family dispute.

A second possibility would be to transfer the shares to a trust for the children. Husband and Wife could be co-trustees and Husband's role in management would be protected. We will discuss the use of these kind of trusts in more detail in Chapters Seven and Eight.

As a third alternative, the shares of the corporation could be placed in a Family Limited Partnership, with Husband and Wife as co-general partners. This arrangement would provide excellent protection for the corporate shares. This strategy is discussed in greater detail in Chapter Eight.

Assuming that the corporate shares are successfully protected from creditors, the corporation would be effective in shielding personal assets from claims. It should be noted that this corporation cannot engage in any business actively, because if the corporation is sued, all of the assets would then be placed at risk. Instead, this corporation would be a passive holding company. Business activity would have to be conducted by another entity.

A major drawback to this arrangement is that the tax treatment of corporations is much more cumbersome than the tax treatment of partnerships, and using corporations to hold personal assets can produce some hazardous and unintended tax consequences. Although an S Corporation produces a result similar to a partnership, the Internal Revenue Code does not permit a partnership or an irrevocable trust to own shares of an S Corporation. Because of the potentially negative tax consequences, most of the time we conclude that the Family Limited Partnership is superior to a corporation when intended solely for asset protection purposes.

Asset Protection Scams

There are a number of companies and individuals promoting the use of Nevada corporations to "judgment proof" one's wealth. This so called strategy involves the formation of two corporations, one in a person's home state ("Home State") and one in Nevada ("Nevada Corp."). Home State holds all business and personal assets. Nevada Corp. "loans" money to Home State for which it receives a lien on all of Home State's assets. This makes it appear as if Home State has no equity — nothing to be reached by a creditor.

The problem with this approach is that a creditor will reach the shares which the individual owns in Nevada Corp. and Home State. He will then own both corporations and he can proceed to liquidate them and reach all of the assets.

The only way that such a plan could conceivably work would be if the debtor denied owning the shares of Nevada Corp. Then, if the creditor was not aware of the "secret" ownership held by the debtor, it would indeed appear as if Home State had no equity in its assets. However, since the debtor will be questioned under oath about his financial affairs, in order to carry out this ruse the debtor will be committing perjury, which is a criminal offense. Needless to say, an asset protection strategy which relies on criminal conduct for success is not an approach which will be useful to anyone with any common sense.

SUMMARY

We have seen that the corporation will provide significant benefits by limiting the liability of business owners from particular sources of lawsuits. A corporation will be especially effective in situations involving negligence claims and disputes with customers. However, lawsuit protection will be lost if the corporate entity is disregarded by the courts. In order to maintain the sanctity of the corporation as a separate and distinct entity, proper minutes and accounting records must be maintained and correspondence and contracts with third parties must clearly establish that it is the corporation and not the individual which is conducting the business.

Corporate assets can and should be protected through a variety of asset protection strategies. Personal assets can be protected by transferring them to a corporation. This arrangement often causes a variety of income tax problems but may be useful under certain circumstances. The shares must be then held by an entity such as the Family Limited Partnership or some form of trust in order to prevent a creditor from seizing the stock.

WHEN TO USE A CORPORATION

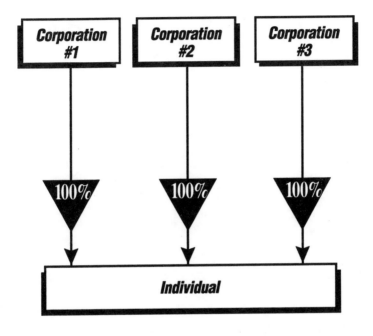

Figure 6-1

WHEN TO USE A CORPORATION

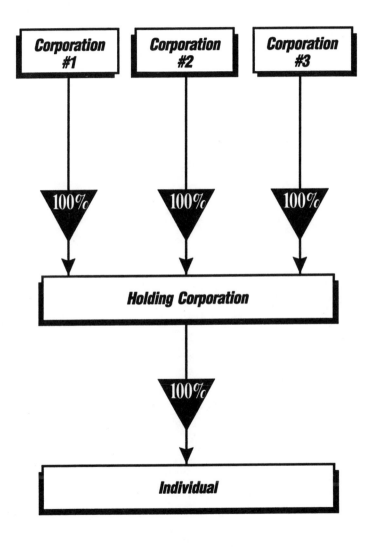

Figure 6-2

WHEN TO USE A CORPORATION

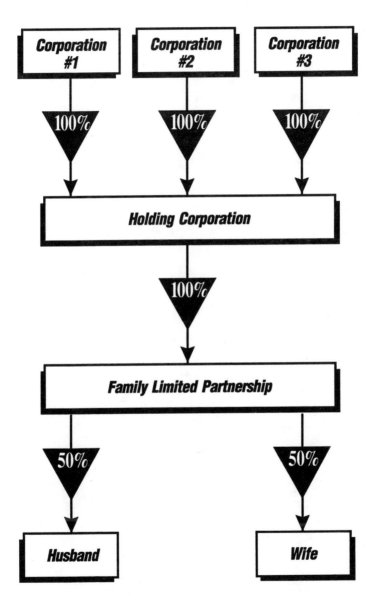

Figure 6-3

ASSET PROTECTION WITH TRUSTS AND GIFTS

Various strategies involving trusts and gifts will be extremely effective in creating an asset protection plan. This Chapter will provide a background for understanding how these techniques work.

The legal arrangement which is known as a trust has been around for at least several hundred years. Every trust has certain essential characteristics. A trust has one or more *trustees,* who are responsible for administering and carrying out the terms of the trust. The *beneficiaries* are those who are entitled to trust income or principle currently or at some time in the future. A trust is typically in a form of a written trust agreement between the *settlor*, the person creating the trust, and the trustee. The written trust agreement provides that the settlor will transfer certain assets to the trustee and the trustee will hold those assets for the benefit of the named beneficiaries.

Until recently, trusts were used almost exclusively by the wealthiest families in order to maintain privacy and to pass their wealth from generation to generation. The proper use of trusts, combined with particular gift giving techniques, provides an excellent means of accomplishing certain estate planning objectives and will also play an important role in creating an asset protection strategy.

UNDERSTANDING YOUR REVOCABLE TRUST

A revocable living trust is a trust that can be revoked or canceled at any time by the settlor. The term "living trust" means simply that the trust is established during the lifetime of the settlor. During the past ten or fifteen years revocable trusts have gained enormous popularity. At least one best selling book has been written and many attorneys and insurance salesmen conduct seminars in every city extolling the virtues of this device. Claims are made that the revocable trust can accomplish everything from saving income and estate taxes to preserving the husband's assets in the event of a divorce. Unfortunately, the client often does not have the slightest idea what the revocable trust does or whether it accomplishes his personal estate planning objectives. The revocable trust is a good device for accomplishing a number of legitimate estate planning goals—but its benefits and limitations must be fully appreciated.

Avoiding Probate

A revocable trust (or irrevocable trust) which is properly drafted and funded will avoid probate. This is the most significant and valuable feature of a revocable trust. The benefits of avoiding probate can only be appreciated by understanding what happens when an estate must be probated.

If a person dies owning property, not protected by a trust, a court will supervise the transfer of that property to those people named in his will. If someone dies without a will, his property passes to his relatives in the manner set forth under the laws of his state. The actual transfer of title to the decedent's property is carried out under the court's supervision by a person designated in the will as the *Executor* of the estate. If a person dies without a will, the court must appoint an *Administrator* to carry out the transfer of the decedent's property. An Executor or Administrator is known as a Personal Representative.

The Personal Representative has the responsibility to perform the following acts:

- Locate, inventory, and appraise all of the assets of the decedent

- Make final payment to all of the decedent's creditors

- Prepare and file any federal and state death tax returns; and

- Distribute the assets of the decedent's estate according to the decedent's will or according to state law

The Personal Representative will almost always hire an attorney to perform this work on his behalf. The attorneys collect their fees from the estate for these services. The amount of legal fees, depending upon the state, is either a fixed percentage of the estate or is based upon what a judge determines to be a reasonable fee.

The reason that most people do not want their estate to go through probate is that this process is expensive, time consuming and inconvenient. Attorney's fees may range from 2% to 10% of the gross value of the estate. An estate of $1,000,000, depending upon the complications involved, may incur attorney's fees of $25,000. These fees are usually based upon the gross value of the estate rather than the net value. An estate of $1,000,000 with $950,000 of liabilities might still pay attorneys fees of $25,000. But now this amount is 50%, not 2 1/2% of the net value.

Second, attorneys rarely feel the same sense of urgency about completing the probate that is felt by the decedent's wife and children. While the decedent's family wishes to get on with things as quickly as possible, the attorney for the estate is often busy handling other matter and the time period for completing the probate may take from two to five years. The entire process causes significant stress and frustration for the survivors. Avoiding the probate procedure is a legitimate concern for anyone familiar with the process.

Trustees and Beneficiaries

Revocable trusts are effective in avoiding probate only when the trust document has been properly drafted and only when all of the decedent's property has been previously transferred into the trust prior to his death. The trust document, like a will, provides for the disposition of trust assets upon the death of the settlor. In the typical arrangement, a husband and wife will create a revocable trust with both husband and wife as the initial trustees. They are also the beneficiaries of the trust. The trust provides that during their joint lifetimes the trust may be revoked at any time. Upon the death of either spouse, the trust typically becomes irrevocable and the trust property passes according to the decedent's wishes.

Funding the Trust

In order for the revocable trust to be effective in eliminating probate, it is essential that all family assets be transferred into the trust prior to a spouse's death. Any property that has not been transferred into the trust will be subject to probate, defeating the purpose of creating the trust in the first place. An amazing number of people go to the trouble and expense of forming a revocable trust and then fail to complete the work necessary to fund it.

Funding the trust involves transferring legal title from husband and wife into the name of the trust. For example, if Harry and Martha Jones are funding their revocable trust, they will change title to their assets from "Harry Jones and Martha Jones, husband and wife" to "Harry Jones and Martha Jones as Trustees of the Jones Family Trust, Dated _____, 1994."

For real estate, the change in title is accomplished by executing and recording a deed to the property. Bank accounts and brokerage accounts can be transferred by simply changing the name on the accounts. Shares of stock and bonds in registered form are changed by notifying the transfer agent for the issuing company and requesting that the certificates be re-issued in the name of the trust. Stock in a family owned corporation can be changed by endorsing the old stock certificate over to the trust and having the corporation issue a new certificate to the trust. Other types of property can be transferred by a simple written declaration called an Assignment.

Death Taxes

The trust must also contain the appropriate provisions in order to minimize federal taxes payable upon the death of either spouse. It is important to point out that death taxes can be minimized with either a properly drawn will or a properly drawn revocable trust. The revocable trust does not provide any tax advantages that are not available to a person using a will or some other form of trust in order to accomplish a transfer of his property. But as long as you are using this type of trust to take advantage of its unique features, you should make sure that the estate tax provisions are properly handled.

Federal taxes are imposed on most transfers of property during your lifetime or at the time of your death. Prior to 1977, estate taxes for transfers at death were distinct from gift taxes which were applied to transfers of property during lifetime. The gift tax rate was 75% of the estate tax rate. In 1977 this dual rate structure was abolished and a uniform rate was established for both gift and estate tax purposes. As a result of this change and additional changes in 1981, there is an effective tax exemption of $600,000 for transfers during life or at death. Amounts in excess of $600,000 are taxed at rates ranging from 37% to a maximum of 50% for total transfers exceeding $2,500,000.

The law provides that annual gifts of $10,000 and under are exempt from tax. A husband and wife together can give $20,000 per year. This amount applies to each person to whom a gift is made. So husband and wife could give, as an example, a total of $100,000 per year to their five children and/or grandchildren.

Further, the 1981 law adopted a provision known as the Unlimited Marital Deduction. All amounts transferred between husband and wife, during lifetime or at death, are exempt from tax. This means that if a husband leaves all of his property to his surviving spouse, there will be no estate taxes on his death regardless of the size of his estate. The estate taxes will arise on the death of the second spouse as she transfers her property to her children or other relatives.

Minimizing Taxes

The unified tax credit allows each spouse to transfer up to $600,000 to his children (or anyone else) free of any federal estate taxes. In its simplest form, a properly drawn revocable trust takes advantage of this benefit by providing for the creation of two separate trusts upon the death of the first spouse. These two trusts are referred to as the A trust and the B trust. In a large estate, the B trust will be funded with the first $600,000 of the decedent's estate and the balance will go into the A trust. From the A trust, the surviving spouse will have the right to all income for life plus a power to use any portion of the principal that she so desires. The B trust will generally provide that the surviving spouse is entitled to all income during her life plus the right to use principal for health, education, maintenance, and support. Any amount left in the A trust, in excess of $600,000, at the death of the surviving spouse will be taxable in her estate for estate tax purposes. However, since the surviving spouse is given only limited rights over the B trust, the amount in the B trust will not be taxable in the survivors' estate upon her death. The effect of these provisions is that up to $1,200,000 can be passed from husband and wife to their ultimate beneficiaries without being subject to estate taxes.

At the present time there is considerable sentiment in Congress to reduce this amount from $1,200,000 to $400,000. Such a change would dramatically increase the number of families that would ultimately be exposed to a significant estate tax liability. Because of this potential change in the law, the necessity of careful estate planning to minimize taxes should be a matter of considerable urgency.

Income Tax Treatment of Revocable Trusts

During lifetime, revocable trusts do not provide any income tax savings. For tax purposes the trusts are treated as if they do not exist. A revocable trust is known, for tax purposes, as a *grantor trust*. A grantor trust is not a tax-paying entity. No annual tax return is required to be filed. Instead, all income and loss of the trust is reported on the tax returns of the husband and wife.

Revocable Trusts and Asset Protection

A revocable trust does not provide any protection of assets from judgment creditors. A revocable trust is ignored for creditor purposes just as it is ignored for income tax purposes. In most states, the law provides that if a settlor has the right to revoke the trust, all of the assets are treated as owned by the settlor. Perhaps because of the promotion associated with these trusts, many people mistakenly believe that a revocable trust somehow shields assets from creditors. This is simply not the case. If there is a judgment against you, the creditor is entitled to seize any assets which you have in the trust. Any usefulness which a revocable trust may have in reference to asset protection is discussed below in connection with gifts to a spouse.

WHEN TO MAKE GIFTS

Gifts Between Spouses

As we have stated, gifts between spouses qualify for the Unlimited Marital Deduction which eliminates federal gift taxes on these kind of transfers. The ability to shift the ownership of property between husband and wife without creating a tax liability creates some useful opportunities for achieving valuable asset protection.

Community Property

In community property states each spouse's interest in the community property is subject to the claims of the other spouse's creditors. If there is a judgment against the husband, all community property assets held by husband *and* wife are available to satisfy the judgment. On the other hand, the separate property of a spouse will generally not be subject to the claims of the creditors of the other spouse.

These rules provide some rather obvious opportunities to achieve a measure of asset protection. If community property is divided into equal shares of separate property of the husband and separate property of the wife, those separate property interests will not be available to satisfy the claims of the other spouse's creditor. Those in community property states can at least limit their potential exposure to one-half of the marital property, rather than all of the marital property, by creating this type of division.

The primary drawback of this technique is that a division of community property into separate property may be disadvantageous from an income tax standpoint. All property held as community property receives a stepped-up basis on the death of the first spouse. For example, Husband and Wife buy a property during their marriage for $50,000 that is later worth $100,000. If they sell the property they will have a gain of $50,000 and will pay taxes on that amount. Suppose that instead of selling, the property is held until the time the first spouse dies. All community property now receives a new tax basis equal to its value as of the date of death—$100,000 in this example. Therefore, if the property is held until the death of the first spouse, all taxable gain is eliminated.

This favorable situation does not occur when a husband and wife hold separate property. In this situation only the deceased spouse's interest in the property receives the stepped-up basis. In the above example, if the property were held one-half each by

Husband and Wife, only the interest of the deceased spouse would receive the new basis.

If you hold community property that has substantially appreciated in value, it would probably not be advisable to divide the property into separate shares and thereby lose out on the significant tax savings which can otherwise be achieved. Alternative methods of asset protection should be explored.

SEPARATE PROPERTY

Unequal Division of Property

For those living in states which do not recognize community property, gifts of separate property between a husband and wife can achieve some useful asset protection.

If one spouse is more vulnerable to potential lawsuits than the other spouse, property can simply be transferred by gift from that spouse to the other. For example, if Husband is a physician with a high vulnerability to lawsuits and Wife is a school teacher with low lawsuit vulnerability, property can be transferred by gift from Husband to Wife in order to reduce the amount of assets subject to loss in the event of a lawsuit. In theory, all assets could be moved out of the name of Husband and into the name of Wife. In the event of a subsequent lawsuit and judgment against Husband, no assets would be available in order to satisfy the creditor.

The advantage of this gift technique is that it is simple and inexpensive to utilize. Property is simply deeded from one spouse to the other. A gift from husband to wife does not create any gift tax liability because of the unlimited marital deductions for gifts between spouses.

One disadvantage of this technique is that if the husband continues to enjoy the use and benefits of the property, it is likely that a court would find that an "implied trust" has been created. The risk is that a court might find that the property transferred to the wife was intended by the parties to be held by the wife for the joint use of the couple during their marriage. As such, the husband's interest as a beneficiary in this implied trust could be seized by his creditors.

The second major problem with this technique is that, in almost all cases, a spouse will be extremely reluctant to relinquish all effective control over his property. If all family assets, including real estate and bank accounts are in the sole name of the wife, the husband may not feel comfortable with this arrangement. The threat of a potential lawsuit, sometime in the future, will rarely be sufficient to overcome the desire to maintain at least equal management and control over one's property.

The third problem is that in the event of a divorce a court may be unwilling to rearrange any bona-fide transfers previously made between husband and wife. Although a court in a dissolution proceeding has broad equitable powers to divide marital assets in a fair and just manner, property which was the subject of a bona-fide gift from husband to wife may or may not be reallocated by a judge. In our practice, we have found that most clients are not willing to risk the possibility that they will be permanently deprived of assets previously transferred to the other spouse.

Lastly, despite the fact that the wife has a low level of lawsuit vulnerability associated with her work, the fact remains that there are numerous ways she could still be sued. Remember, as the owner of substantial assets she becomes an inviting target for a lawsuit. Putting all of your eggs in this basket is a dangerous proposition.

Equal Division of Property

An equal division of marital property, as opposed to a strict transfer from one spouse to the other might provide greater lawsuit protection and might also allow each spouse to sleep more easily. Marital property can be divided according to a written agreement which states that each spouse is to hold one-half of all marital property as their own separate property. This is where a revocable trust may become particularly useful for our purposes. Once the marital property is divided, two separate revocable trusts can be established, one for each spouse. The husband's trust then holds title to his one-half of the property and the wife's trust holds title to her one-half interest.

When marital property is divided in this manner, a number of our previous concerns can be eliminated. First, when property is held pursuant to a written trust agreement, it is unlikely that a court would imply the existence of some other type of trust arrangement which is not consistent with the terms of the written trust. It is therefore unlikely that a court would allow a creditor of the husband to reach into and claim the property held in the wife's revocable trust on the theory that she is holding that property for the benefit of her husband. As a result, property held by the wife in her trust would be removed from potential claims from the husband's creditors. Although the property in the husband's trust would still be available for these creditors' claims, at least one-half of the total estate has been removed from the reach of the husband's creditors. Admittedly this is only a partial solution to the problem, but it is a useful beginning.

This arrangement also minimizes concerns about losing management and control over one's assets. The husband would still have full management and control over the assets in his revocable trust and, in the event of a divorce, each spouse is likely to have no more property than they would otherwise be entitled to.

GIFTS TO OTHER FAMILY MEMBERS

Making gifts of property to family members is a useful tool which may accomplish a variety of asset protection objectives. A properly structured program of gift giving, to one's children or grandchildren, can result in a minimization of estate and income taxes and can also be useful for achieving a significant degree of lawsuit protection.

Tax Savings and Lawsuit Protection

As previously discussed, there are significant advantages to a gift giving program. Lifetime gifts reduce the size of one's estate and consequently minimize the ultimate amount of estate taxes. Since estate tax rates are very high, substantial savings will be realized from this technique. Using up the $600,000 unified credit may also make good sense if Congress decides to reduce or eliminate the credit in an effort to cut down the federal deficit.

A gift giving program may also produce some annual income tax savings. If a donee is fourteen years or older, income which is earned on the property transferred to him will be taxable to the child rather than to the parent. If a child is in a lower income tax bracket then the parent, a gift program will effectively spread the income tax liability of the family among lower bracket tax-payers and will thereby reduce the overall income tax burden.

A gift program also provides significant lawsuit protection. If a gift transfer does not violate the fraudulent conveyance laws, property which has been transferred to a child or a grandchild cannot be reached by a judgment creditor of the husband or wife. Once an effective gift has been made from a parent to a child, this asset cannot be seized by the parents' creditors.

Drawbacks of Outright Gifts

The most obvious difficulty with outright gifts is the total loss of ownership and control of the gifted property. In our years of legal practice, we have rarely encountered instances in which parents are willing to transfer complete control over large sums of money to their children. Despite considerable estate and income tax savings, very few people are willing to give up a portion of their wealth which they have worked hard to accumulate during their lifetime.

Even when their wealth is beyond what they reasonably need to live comfortably, parents are concerned about the wisdom of making outright gifts to their children. Sometimes there is an issue concerning the child's marital status and what will happen to the gifted property in the event the child is divorced. Sometimes there are concerns about the child's level of financial responsibility and whether the funds will be squandered. Many times the parents are concerned about the creditors of a child reaching the property. When the situation involves minor children or grandchildren, who are not legally capable of holding a title to property, there are questions about who will act on the child's behalf in holding the property and when the property should be distributed to the child. These are all matters of great consequence and must be carefully considered by parents contemplating this type of gift giving program. In Chapter Eight we will explore how the Family Limited Partnership will be useful in creating a gift program that will accomplish a variety of objectives, without the disadvantages commonly associated with a traditional gift program.

HOW TO USE IRREVOCABLE TRUSTS

Some additional problems of an outright gift giving program can be eliminated or mitigated through the use of an irrevocable trust. The distinguishing feature of an irrevocable trust is, as the name implies, that the trust cannot be revoked or canceled by the settlor. The irrevocable trust is a written agreement between the settlor and the trustee in which the trustee agrees to hold property transferred by the settlor on behalf of certain specified beneficiaries.

Typically, the beneficiaries will be the children or grandchildren. The parents will transfer to the trust the annual exclusion amount of $20,000 per year for each beneficiary. If the parents' estate is large enough and they can afford to do so, they may make a larger gift, using all or a portion of their combined $1,200,000 unified tax credit. The greater the amount of the gift, the more significant will be the estate tax, income tax and lawsuit protection achievements.

Advantages of the Irrevocable Trust

The irrevocable trust solves a number of problems posed by the outright gift giving program. If the parents are the trustees, even if they have transferred substantial assets into the trust, they will still enjoy the management and control over that property. Although the trustees cannot use the property for their own benefit, they may retain some degree of discretion regarding the investment of trust asset and the amount and timing of any distributions to the beneficiaries. This ability to maintain effective control over the transferred property will alleviate one of the parents most frequent concerns.

Second, a child's interest in this kind of a trust can be protected from the child's spouse in the event of a divorce, or from creditors in the event of a judgment. Although the outcome on these issues depends in part upon the law in your particular state and the language which is used in drafting the trust agreement, protection from spouses and potential creditors is a major advantage which can be accomplished using this type of a trust.

The third advantage is that the trust mechanism allows for gifts to be made to minor children or grandchildren. Since minors cannot hold the property in their own name, the use of a trust is essential in order to provide them with the benefits of property ownership and in order to accomplish the gift program.

Tax Savings and Lawsuit Protection

Property which has been transferred to the trust by gift will not be included in the parents' estate when they die. If the transfers begin early enough and continue over a period of years, a significant amount of estate tax savings can be realized. If the parents have, for example, five children and grandchildren, a total of $100,000 per year can be transferred into a trust like this without gift tax consequences. Over a ten year period, $1,000,000 has been removed from the parents' estate. If the parents are in a maximum estate tax bracket of 50%, a total of $500,000 in family wealth will be preserved.

Income tax savings can also be achieved when the trust is in a lower tax bracket than the parents and the beneficiaries are fourteen years or older. An irrevocable trust is a separate tax paying entity, apart from the parents, and the income which the trust earns on its assets is taxable to the trust. Income which is distributed from the trust to a beneficiary is not taxable to the trust, but is instead taxable to the beneficiary. If the parents are in the maximum effective tax bracket and the trust beneficiaries are in lower tax brackets, annual income tax saving can be accomplish through this difference in the tax rates. Over a period of time, this annual tax savings can add up to a substantial amount of money.

The irrevocable trust also provides a significant degree of lawsuit protection for the parents. Because the trust is irrevocable and cannot be canceled or modified in any manner by the parent, and because the parents have no interest in the trust as beneficiaries, property which has been transferred to the trust will be protected from the claims of the parents' creditors.

Factors to Consider

In deciding whether to use an irrevocable trust to accomplish these objectives, there are two primary factors which must be considered. First, this trust cannot be revoked, altered or modified in any manner. Once the parents have transferred property into the trust, it cannot be retrieved. If the financial circumstances of the parents change in the future they still will not be able to reach the property. The parents, must ask themselves: "How much can I afford to transfer?" and "How much do I need to keep to meet my personal needs during my lifetime?" Clearly, if parents transfer all of their assets into the irrevocable trust, the parents must have sufficient income from other sources meet their own needs.

The second important issue is a practical one which involves the manner in which assets are physically transferred to the trust. If the parents' estate consists substantially of investment assets - bank accounts, stocks, and bonds - it is a simple procedure to transfer ownership of those assets to the trust each year. Transfers of real estate or other illiquid assets are more difficult to accomplish.

For example, the parents' major asset may be a piece of commercial real estate. If they wish to make annual gifts to the trust under the annual gift tax exclusion, they will have to deed a fractional interest in the real estate to the trust each year. This can be done but it is a cumbersome process. A greater problem comes from the valuation issues which arise. The parents may consider that the commercial property has an equity of $1,000,000. In order to transfer $20,000 worth of property, they would have to deed a 2% interest. But if the IRS later determined that the actual value of the equity was $1,500,000 rather than $1,000,000, the 2% interest would be equal to $30,000, rather than $20,000 thereby creating a gift tax liability for that year. To avoid this difficulty an annual appraisal of the property can be obtained to provide credible evidence of the actual value on the date of the transfer. However, an appraisal will be relatively expensive and inconvenient, and may still be subject to challenge in the event of a future IRS audit.

SUMMARY

The irrevocable trust is an effective device for reducing estate and income taxes through a program of lifetime gifts to children and grandchildren. Amounts which have been transferred by gift cannot be reached by the parents' creditors, unless the gift is considered to be a fraudulent conveyance. Problems involve the loss of beneficial ownership by the parents and valuation of real estate or illiquid business interests.

In subsequent Chapters we will see how the Family Limited Partnership and the Asset Protection Trust can be used together to eliminate many of the difficulties associated with irrevocable trusts, and how these techniques can be combined to produce the highest degree of total asset protection.

FAMILY LIMITED PARTNERSHIPS

THE WINNING STRATEGY

In this section we will discuss the use of Family Limited Partnerships in accomplishing asset protection objectives. We will see that this type of partnership has features which are superior to any other type of entity. When used correctly, the Family Limited Partnership is the foundation of any plan designed to protect family assets from lawsuits and judgments.

DIFFERENT TYPES OF PARTNERSHIPS

General Partnerships

A partnership is formed when two or more persons agree to carry on a business together. This agreement can be written or oral. A *general partnership* is formed when two or more people intend to work together to carry on a business activity. No local or state filings are required to create this type of partnership. This is different than a corporation which does not come into existence until Articles of Incorporation have been filed with the Secretary of State.

The distinguishing feature of a partnership is the *unlimited liability* of the partners. Each partner is personally liable for all of the debts of the partnership. That includes any debts incurred by any of the other partners on behalf of the partnership. Any one partner is able to bind the partnership by entering into a contract on behalf of the partnership. If Jackson and Wilson are partners, and Wilson signs a contract on behalf of the partnership, Jackson will be personally liable for the full amount. This is true regardless of whether Jackson authorized the contract or whether he even knew of its existence. This feature of unlimited liability contrasts with the limited liability of the owners of a corporation. As discussed previously, when a contract is entered into on behalf of a corporation, the owners are not personally liable for its performance.

Because each of the partners has unlimited personal liability, a general partnership is the single most dangerous form for conducting one's business. Not only is a partner liable for contracts entered into by other partners, each partners is also liable for the other partner's negligence. When two or more physicians or other professionals practice together as a partnership, each partner is liable for the negligence or malpractice of any other partner.

In addition, each partner is personally liable for the *entire* amount of any partnership obligation. For example, Doctor Smith may be one of ten partners in a medical partnership, but he is not responsible for only 10% of partnership obligations. He is responsible for 100% – even though he owns only a 10% interest. If Doctor Smith's other partners are unable to pay their respective shares, he must pay the entire amount.

Limited Partnerships

Obviously, the unlimited liability feature of general partnerships is a serious impediment to conducting business using a partnership format. In order to mitigate the harsh impact of these rules, every state has enacted legislation allowing the formation of a type of partnership known as a *limited partnership.*

A limited partnership consists of one or more *general partners* and one or more *limited partners.* The same person can be both a general partner and a limited partner, as long as there are at least two legal persons who are partners in the partnership. The general partner is responsible for the management of the affairs of the partnership and he has unlimited personal liability for all debts and obligations. Limited partners have no personal liability. The limited partner stands to lose only the amount which he has contributed and any amounts which he has obligated himself to contribute under the terms of the partnership agreement. Limited partnerships are often used as investment vehicles for large projects requiring a considerable amount of cash. Individual limited partners contributing money to a venture, but not having management powers, will not have any personal liability for the debts of the business.

For example, Able and Baker form a limited partnership with Able as the general partner and Baker as the limited partner. Baker contributes $100,000 Able will run the day-to-day affairs of the business and Baker will provide all of the initial capital. If Able enters into a contract which causes the partnership to incur a liability of $500,000, Baker will lose his $100,000 contribution, but he has no obligation to contribute any additional funds. Able, as the general partner, has personal liability for the entire amount. He has no right to demand that Baker make any further contributions.

In exchange for this protection against personal liability, a limited partner may not actively participate in management However, it is permissible for a limited partner to have a vote on certain matters, just as a shareholder has a right to vote on some corporate matters. A typical limited partnership agreement may provide that a majority vote of the limited partners is necessary for the sale of assets or approval may be required in order to remove a general partner. The partnership agreement determines whether the limited partners can vote on these matters.

If a limited partner assumes an active role in management, that partner may lose his limited liability protection and may be treated as a general partner. For instance, if a limited partner negotiates a contract with a third party on behalf of the partnership, the limited partner may have liability as a general partner. For this reason, a limited partner's activities must be carefully circumscribed.

Tax Treatment of Partnerships

Unlike corporations and irrevocable trusts, a partnership is not a taxpaying entity. A partnership files an annual information tax return setting forth its income and expenses, but it doesn't pay tax on its net income. Instead, each partner's proportionate share of income or loss is passed through from the partnership to the individual. Each partner claims his share of deductions or reports his share of income on his own tax return.

Since the partnership is a "pass through" entity, there is no potential for double taxation as there is with a C Corporation. Typically, when a business is expected to show a net loss rather than a gain, the partnership format is used so that the losses can be used by the partners. Limited partnerships have always been used for real estate and tax shelter investments in order to pass the tax deductions through to the individual investors. These losses are then used by the partner to offset other income he might have. Although the Tax Reform Act of 1986 now limits the ability to immediately deduct losses from "passive activities" to offset wages or investment income, the partnership format may still be desirable, if the circumstances of the individual partner are such that he is able to take advantage of these losses.

The rules regarding the taxation of partnership activities are lengthy and cumbersome. As a general rule, however, transfers of property into and out of a partnership ordinarily will not produce any tax consequences.

USING LIMITED PARTNERSHIPS FOR LAWSUIT PROTECTION

The Family Limited Partnership is an outstanding device for providing the highest degree of lawsuit protection for family wealth. When used as part of a properly designed overall strategy, an unsurpassed level of asset protection can be accomplished.

Under the typical arrangement, the FLP is set up so that Husband and Wife are each general partners. As such, they may own only a one or two percent interest in the partnership. The remaining interests are in the form of limited partnership interests. These interests will be held. directly or indirectly, by Husband, Wife or other family members, depending upon a variety of factors which will be discussed.

After setting up the FLP, all family assets are transferred into it, including the family home, investments and business interests. When the transfers are complete, Husband and Wife no longer own a direct interest in these assets. Instead, they own a controlling interest in the FLP and it is the FLP which owns the assets. As general partners, they have complete management and control over the affairs of the partnership and can buy or sell any assets they wish. They have the right to retain in the partnership proceeds from the sale of any partnership assets or they can distribute these proceeds out to the partners.

Creditor Cannot Reach Assets

Now, let us see what happens if there is a lawsuit against either Husband or Wife. Assume that Husband is a physician and that there is a malpractice judgment against him for $1,000,000. The plaintiff in the action is now a judgment creditor and he will try to collect the $1,000,000 from Husband.

The judgment creditor would like to seize Husband's bank accounts, investments and even the family home in order to collect the amount which he is owed. However, he discovers that Husband no longer holds title to any of these assets. In fact, since all of these assets have been transferred to the FLP, the only asset held by Husband is his interest in the FLP. Can the creditor reach into the partnership and seize the family home, investments and bank accounts?

The answer is no. Under the provisions of the Uniform Limited Partnership Act, *a creditor of a partner cannot reach into the partnership and take specific partnership assets.* The creditor has no rights to any property which is held by the partnership. Since title to the assets is in the name of the partnership and it is the Husband partner rather than the partnership which is liable for the debt, partnership assets may not be taken to satisfy the judgment.

Charging Order Remedy

If a judgment creditor cannot reach partnership assets, what can he do? Since Husband's only asset is an interest in the FLP, the creditor would apply to the court for a *charging order* against Husband's partnership interest. A charging order means that the general partner is directed to pay over to the judgment creditor any distributions from the partnership which would otherwise go the debtor partner, until the judgment is paid in full. In other words, money which comes out of the partnership to the debtor partner can be seized by the creditor until the amount of the judgment is satisfied. Cash distributions paid to Husband could, therefore, be taken by the creditor. A charging order does *not* give the creditor the right to become a partner in the partnership and does *not* give him any right to interfere in the management or control of partnership affairs. All he gets is the right to any actual distributions paid to Husband.

Under the circumstances in which a creditor has obtained a charging order, the partnership would not make any distributions to the debtor partner. This arrangement would be provided for in the partnership agreement and is permissible under partnership law. If the partnership does not make any distributions the judgment creditor will not receive any payments. The partnership simply retains all of its funds and continues to invest and reinvest its cash without making any distributions.

The result of this technique is that family assets have been successfully protected from the judgment against Husband. Had the FLP arrangement not been used and had Husband and Wife kept all of their assets in their own names, the judgment creditor would have seized everything. Instead, through the use of this technique, all of these assets were protected.

Reason For This Law

The law prohibiting a creditor from reaching the assets of the partnership has been well established for many years. In fact, these particular provisions of partnership law were first adopted as part of the English Partnership Act of 1890 and were subsequently adopted as part of the Uniform Partnership Act which has been the basis of the law in the United States since the 1940s.

The reason for these provisions is that they are necessary to accomplish a particular public policy objective. This policy is that the business activities of a partnership should not be disrupted because of non-partnership related debts of one of the partners. Prior to the adoption of these provisions it was possible for a creditor of a partner to obtain a Writ of Execution ordering the local sheriff to levy directly on the property of the partnership to satisfy the creditor's debt. The local sheriff went to the partnership's place of business, shut down the business, seized all of the assets and sold them to satisfy the debt. These methods not only destroyed the partnership's business but also caused a significant economic injustice to the non-debtor partner through the forced liquidation of partnership assets. The non-debtor partner didn't do anything wrong. Why should he be forced to suffer?

In order to avoid precisely these unfair results, the law was formulated so that a creditor with a judgment against a partner—but not against the partnership—cannot execute directly on partnership assets. Instead, the law allows the creditor to obtain a charging order which affects only the actual distributions made to the debtor partner. The business of the partnership is allowed to continue unhampered and the economic interest of the non-debtor partner is not impaired.

The protection of partnership assets from the claims of one partner's creditors is deeply entrenched in the foundation of American and English partnership law. Without such protection the formation of partnerships would be discouraged and legitimate business activities would be impeded. When understood in this light, it is clear that the asset protection features of a Family Limited Partnership are neither a fluke nor a loop hole in the law. Rather, these provisions are an integral part of partnership design and it is unlikely that changes in the law will ever be made which would impair these features.

WHO SHOULD HOLD INTERESTS IN THE PARTNERSHIP

A decision must be made concerning who should own the limited partnership interests in the Family Limited Partnership. Under the arrangement which we have proposed, Husband and Wife are general partners, each owning a 1% interest. The question is who should own the remaining 98%? There are several possibilities to consider.

Husband and Wife Own Limited Partnership Interests

The first alternative is that Husband and Wife could own all or most of the limited partnership interests. It is perfectly acceptable for the same person to be both a general partner and a limited partner. The Uniform Limited Partnership Act specifically sanctions this set-up.

The advantage of this arrangement is that it is attractive and convenient. The parents fully control all partnership assets by virtue of their powers as general partners. In addition, the parents have retained most of the equity through their ownership of the limited partnership interests. This arrangement is generally consistent with the parents' desire not to part with assets in any meaningful way.

The disadvantages of this format are that the equitable interests retained by the parents may open the door to particular remedies which can be employed by a potential creditor. These remedies are the charging order and a possible foreclosure of the partnership interests.

Foreclosure Remedy

We have previously discussed the fact that a judgment creditor of a partner can obtain a charging order against the debtor's partnership interest. A charging order does not give a creditor any right to participate in partnership affairs, nor does it give him any right to demand payments from the partnership. A charging order does give the creditor a right to receive the debtor partner's share of any distributions made by the partnership. The charging order stays in effect until the creditor has been paid in full or until the time limit for collecting the judgment has expired (usually 20 years).

Traditionally, the charging order has been the sole remedy of the creditor. Recently, however, there has been a movement to allow a creditor with an unsatisfied charging order to obtain a *foreclosure* of the debtor partner's interest. A foreclosure means that the court allows a seizure and a sale of the debtor's partnership interest. Just like with a charging order, the purchaser of the partnership interest would not become a partner and would not have any right to interfere in partnership affairs. A creditor still would not have any right to seize any of the assets of the partnership. The difference between a charging order and a foreclosure is that a creditor with a charging order would be entitled to distributions only to the extent of the judgment. A creditor who has foreclosed on a partnership interest would be entitled to the debtor's share of distributions without regard to the amount of the judgment.

For example, a creditor with a $100,000 judgment must release his charging order when he has been paid the full amount of the judgment. If the creditor instead forecloses on the partnership interest, he will be entitled to all distributions, regardless of the amount, for the life of the partnership.

As a practical matter, the partnership may never make any actual distributions and the creditor would not receive anything under either a charging order or a foreclosure. Alternatively, the general partner may dissipate the assets of the partnership such that an interest held by a creditor becomes worthless. It is not clear what relief a court would offer a creditor under those circumstances.

Crocker and *Hellman* Cases

Two California courts have interpreted California partnership law in a way which sanctions a court ordered foreclosure of a debtor partner's interest under certain circumstances. In the 1989 case of *Crocker National Bank* the court held that a foreclosure of a debtor partner's interest was permissible if three requirements were met:

1. The creditor must have a judgment against the partner
2. The creditor must have an unsatisfied charging order; and
3. The non-debtor partners must consent

At least in the context of a Family Limited Partnership, the rule in *Crocker* would not cause any concern. The requirement that all partners must consent to a foreclosure would present an obvious impediment, since other family member partners would not be expected to consent to this action.

However, in a 1991 case, before a different appellate circuit, the court disagreed with the consent rule established in *Crocker*. In *Hellman v. Anderson,* the court held that the consent of the other partners was not a prerequisite to foreclosure of a partnership interest. Instead, the court adopted the rule that a foreclosure was permissible, unless it would impair the ability of the partnership to carry on its business. An example presented by the court of this type of impairment involves the foreclosure of a general partner's interest. If the services provided by that partner were essential to the conduct of partnership business, a foreclosure would not be warranted if the effect of the foreclosure would be to deprive the partnership of the services of that partner.

If is difficult to predict exactly how the law on this matter will be resolved. Because of the disagreement between the two appellate circuits in *Crocker* and *Hellman,* the issue may have to be resolved by the California Supreme Court. It will also be interesting to see how other state courts approach this question and whether the *Hellman* decision begins a trend that will ultimately prevail throughout the country.

In light of the *Hellman* case, and anticipating that ultimately it may become the established rule throughout the country, Husband and Wife should not hold most of the limited partnership interests in their names. Since partnership interests held by

Husband or Wife are subject to charging order and possibly foreclosure, various alternatives should be explored which would remove the partnership interests from the danger of a possible foreclosure.

Transfer to Less Vulnerable Spouse

If one spouse is more vulnerable then the other to potential lawsuits allowing the less vulnerable spouse to hold the partnership interests may be one useful technique. For example, let's use the situation again where Husband is a physician with high potential liability and Wife is a school teacher with low potential liability. Both Husband and Wife would be general partners, each with a 1% interest. But instead of dividing the limited partnership shares equally, all of the limited partnership interests would be held by Wife. If Wife's partnership interests were considered to be her separate property (not community property), a judgment creditor of the Husband could only get a charging order or a foreclosure against the 1% interest held by Husband. Although Husband still enjoys co-equal management and control of the family assets as co-general partner, he has effectively parted with beneficial ownership so that potential creditors are left without a means for recovery. In the event of a charging order or foreclosure, the creditor will only be able to reach the 1% general partnership interest retained by Husband. The other 99% will be protected. This technique will not produce any gift tax consequences, because of the unlimited marital deductions for gifts between spouses.

This arrangement will also be useful if the income

from partnership assets is essential for the support of the family. For instance, the assets of the partnership may consist of retirement savings, the income from which is used to pay family living expenses. If a creditor obtains a judgment and the right to any distributions, money cannot be distributed to a debtor partner without being seized by the creditor. Instead, if the debtor partner owns only a 1% interest as general partner, the creditor could claim only 1% of any distributions. Distributions made to Wife, who is not a debtor partner, would not be available for the creditor. In our example, Wife owns 99%, allowing 99% of the partnership income to be distributed to her free of the creditors claim.

The primary disadvantage of this technique is that a low vulnerability to lawsuits does not mean no vulnerability. It is often very difficult to determine where and when an accident may occur or liability may arise. In this example, a lawsuit against Wife would be disastrous because of her ownership of all of the limited partnership interests. Also, again, transfers of all interests to Wife will certainly cause problems in the event of a divorce.

Transfers to Children

Sometimes, Husband and Wife are equally vulnerable to lawsuits or Husband doesn't feel comfortable transferring to his spouse all of the beneficial interests in the partnership. In circumstances where partnership assets do not generate income or distributions are not necessary for family support, a transfer of the partnership interests to the children is a technique to consider. An irrevocable domestic trust would be a method to accomplish this. Husband and Wife could be the trustees of the trust, but under the law of most states they could not have any beneficial interest in the trust if they wished to protect the partnership interests from a possible creditor.

Gift Tax Consequences

In establishing such a trust, the parents must keep in mind potential gift tax consequences. If the transfer of the partnership interests to the trust is considered to be a completed gift, it may give rise to current gift tax liability, depending upon how the interests are valued. The parents may use up their combined credits against tax which total $1,200,000 without incurring any immediate tax liability. And, as discussed, annual transfers of partnership interests with a value of $20,000 per donee can be made.

If Husband and Wife own property with a value greater than $1,200,00, it may be difficult to make an immediate transfer of all of the partnership interests to a trust without triggering a gift tax liability. For example, if Husband and Wife have three children and no grandchildren, the most that can be transferred in the first year is $1,260,000.

Incomplete Gifts

In order to transfer amounts over $1,200,000 without gift tax, a trust arrangement can be created which is not considered to be a completed gift for gift tax purposes. Although the trust is irrevocable and the transfer is complete under state law with respect to potential creditors, a gift can still be incomplete for tax purposes. An incomplete gift occurs when the donor retains some significant powers over the gifted property. Even if the donor cannot re-acquire the property and cannot enjoy the property himself, if he is able to exercise significant control over the property, the gift will be considered incomplete. For example, if a donor retains a right to add beneficiaries to the trust or to alter the interests of the beneficiaries, the transfer would not be a completed gift and no gift tax liability would be created. Similarly, for income tax purposes the trust can be structured so that all of the income tax attributes of the property are retained by the donor. In essence, the trust would be treated as a grantor trust, in the same manner as the revocable trust. If Husband and Wife wish to protect the interests in the partnership without incurring any gift tax liability, the incomplete gift technique is an excellent method for doing so.

Advantages and Disadvantages of Irrevocable Trust

Partnership interests which have been transferred to an irrevocable trust are immune from charging order or foreclosure. The parents, as general partners of the partnership and trustees of the trust, have retained complete control over the assets of the partnership and the timing and amount of any distributions to the children. If the transfer takes the form of a completed gift, the value of the partnership interests will not be includable in the estate of the parents. This can be a very effective estate planning maneuver.

The major disadvantage is that the parents have, in fact, irrevocably parted with legal ownership of the interests in the partnership. As general partners and trustees, they are bound by the laws of the state to carry out their responsibilities in a fiduciary capacity. That is, the parents now have a legal obligation to administer the partnership and the trust, not in their own self interest but in the best interest of the children. If partnership assets are wasted or if the general partners receive excessive compensation, the children will have a legal cause of action for damages. These facts may or may not cause concern. Many of our clients are completely comfortable with this type of arrangement and do not view a potential lawsuit from their children as a serious possibility.

Asset Protection Trusts

For those people who are reluctant to create an irrevocable trust and relinquish all beneficial ownership to their children, a trust established under the more favorable laws of a foreign jurisdiction will provide a satisfactory solution to these concerns. In the next Chapter, we will examine how Asset Protection Trusts can be used in conjunction with the Family Limited Partnership to provide the ultimate asset protection strategy.

HOW TO SAVE INCOME AND ESTATE TAXES

Income Tax Benefits

If family assets are held in the form of a limited partnership, it will be possible to obtain certain income tax savings in addition to the asset protection benefits previously discussed. These income tax benefits can be realized by spreading income from high tax bracket parents to lower tax bracket children and grandchildren who are 14 years or older. Let's look at an example of how this might work:

One of our clients had taxable income from various investments of approximately $200,000, consisting of interest and dividends from bonds, stocks, and trust deeds which he owned. He was in a 32% maximum tax bracket and paid taxes of approximately $64,000 per year on this income. As part of an overall business plan which we established, all of his assets were transferred into a Family Limited Partnership and a total of seven children and grandchildren were brought in as limited partners of the partnership. Under the partnership agreement, the children and grandchildren were taxable on $100,000 of the $200,000 in income generated by the partnership. Each of these children was in a maximum tax bracket of 15% and thus the total taxes owed on this $100,000 of investment income was reduced from $32,000 to $15,000. This produced a savings of $17,000 in overall family income taxes. Under the partnership agreement it was not required that the $100,000 actually be distributed to the children. In fact, the parents as general partners retained all of this amount except for what was needed to pay the taxes on the children's share of partnership income. The parents thereby reduced their annual income taxes by shifting a substantial amount of income to their children. The tax savings were held as a college fund for the grandchildren.

Estate Tax Benefits

We have devoted a considerable amount of attention to the usefulness of the Family Limited Partnership for various asset protection strategies. However, the importance of the FLP as a vehicle for dramatically reducing or eliminating estate taxes must not be overlooked.

This estate tax reduction can be accomplished because of certain unique attributes of the FLP which are not present in any other business entity. Of primary importance is the ability to shift the value of assets out of your estate without any concomitant loss of control, through a program of gifting limited partnership interests to your children or other family members.

For example, the Smith family has equity in a home of $500,000, a rental property with equity of $500,000 and retirement savings in stocks and bonds equal to $1,000,000. Under current law, a properly designed estate plan, taking maximum advantage of the $600,000 exemptions, would result in an estate tax of approximately $400,000. Congress is also considering new proposals which would reduce the amount of the lifetime exemption from $600,000 per person to only $200,000. Under the new proposals the amount of estate tax would equal approximately $800,000. Mr. and Mrs. Smith would like to take steps to preserve the family estate for the benefit of their three children but they do not wish to give up control over their assets during their lifetime.

The solution to the problem involves a properly structured estate plan including an FLP which is established to hold all family assets. Mr. and Mrs. Smith would be the general partners of the FLP. As such they would have complete management and control over their property in the FLP. Initially, they could make a gift of the limited partnership interests to their children in an amount equal in value to the combined maximum estate tax credit (currently $1,200,000). In subsequent years they could gift limited partnership interests equal to the amount of the annual gift tax exclusion of $20,000 per child ($60,000 per year).

Under this approach, in roughly 13 years, the Smiths would be able to eliminate potential estate taxes and could preserve $400,000 to $800,000 of family wealth. At the same time that the Smiths are accomplishing this result they would not relinquish any degree of control or authority over their real-estate or their retirement savings.

A further advantage to using the FLP in this manner is that according to IRS regulations, the value of each gift of a limited partnership interest must be discounted in order to account for the lack of marketability and the lack of control associated with those interests. For example, if the parents transfer assets with a value of $1,000,000 to an FLP, a gift of a one percent limited partnership interest should not be valued at $10,000. Instead, because the interest cannot be readily sold and because the donee has no right to participate in management of the FLP, a reasonable approach to determine value, suggested by many financial advisors, would be to discount the transferred interest by approximately thirty percent.

Once this discount is taken into consideration, the value of the gifted interests is reduced from $10,000 to $7,000. By valuing these interests at this reduced amount, a greater amount can be gifted each year. In the example that we used above, the Smiths could reduce their taxable estate to zero in only 9 years by discounting the value of the gifted interests in this manner.

From a practical standpoint a transfer of a limited partnership interest is easy and convenient to accomplish. A simple notation may be made in the partnership document reflecting a decrease in the parents' ownership and an increase in the children's ownership. This procedure is simpler than transferring a fractional interest in an asset, such as real estate, which would require the preparation of a new deed each year to reflect the correct ownership percentage held by the children. If a trust has been used to hold the limited partnership interests, annual transfers can be accomplished by an assignment, of the desired percentage from the trust to the beneficiary each year.

The Family Limited Partnership is the best legal device available for minimizing or eliminating estate taxes through the transfer of ownership to other family members. The ability of the parents to maintain control over the assets and the administrative ease with which these transfers are accomplished makes this device superior to any other available technique for accomplishing these objectives.

CREATING THE FAMILY LIMITED PARTNERSHIP

The first step in creating the Family Limited Partnership is the preparation and filing of the Certificate of Limited Partnership with the Secretary of State in your state. The form asks for the name of the limited partnership. This name should be cleared in advance with the office of the Secretary of State, because the filing will not be accepted if the name is similar to another name already on file. Making sure that your partnership name is available will avoid the inconvenience of having your Certificate of Limited Partnership returned unfiled. You will then have to select a new name and go through the process again. Calling the office of the Secretary of State in advance to confirm the availability of your chosen name will avoid this inconvenience and will expedite the process.

The Certificate of Limited Partnership also asks for the name of a designated Agent for the Service of Process, which is the name and address of a person (or company) who is authorized by the partnership to receive service of process, if the partnership is sued for any reason. Any family member residing in the state can be designated as the agent. There are also companies which will, for a modest fee, act as the designated agent for these purposes.

The form also asks for the names and addresses of all general partners of the partnership. The names of the limited partners are not required. Since this document is a matter of public record, the names of the general partners will be publicly available but not the names of the limited partners. Along with the Certificate of Limited Partnership, each state requires a filing fee which is usually about $85-$125.

When the properly filled out form with an acceptable partnership name is received by the office of the Secretary of State, the Certificate will be filed. At this point, the partnership will be legally formed. You should request that a certified copy of the Certificate of Limited Partnership be returned to you and your copy should be stamped with the filing date. It is essential that you have at least one certified copy for opening a bank account or brokerage account, or, if you buy or sell real estate in the name of the partnership.

The Partnership Agreement

Concurrently with the filing of the Certificate of Limited Partnership, a written partnership agreement must be prepared. This is the document that governs the affairs of the partnership. It sets out the purpose of the partnership; the duties of the general partners; matters on which the vote of the limited partners is required; the share of partnership capital and profits to which each partner is entitled; and all other matters affecting the relations between the partners.

When creating a Family Limited Partnership for estate planning and asset protection purposes, the partnership agreement must also contain certain key provisions designed to accomplish your objectives. Taken together, these provisions must insure that a creditor can never achieve any influence over partnership affairs and that Husband and Wife, as general partners, always maintain absolute control over the assets of the partnership. These provisions are unique and essential to a properly structured Family Limited Partnership.

FUNDING THE PARTNERSHIP

The next step in the partnership formation process is the funding of the partnership. That means you must now decide which assets to transfer and the best means for doing so.

Dangerous and Safe Assets

In making the decision about funding the partnership it is vitally important that you understand the distinction between *Safe Assets* and *Dangerous Assets*.

Safe Assets are those which do not, by themselves, produce a high degree of lawsuit risk. For instance, if you own investment securities such as stocks, bonds or mutual funds, it is unlikely that these assets will cause you to be sued. Mere ownership of investment assets, without some active involvement in the underlying business, would probably not cause a significant degree of lawsuit exposure.

Dangerous Assets, on the other hand, are those which, by their nature, create a substantial risk of liability. These are generally active business type assets, or even motor vehicles or aircraft, the ownership of which may cause you to be sued.

The reason for the distinction between Safe Assets and Dangerous Assets is that you do not wish to have the partnership incur liability because of its ownership of a Dangerous Asset. If the partnership does incur liability, it will be the target of a lawsuit and all of the assets in that partnership will be subject to the claims of the judgment creditor. This is exactly the situation you are trying to avoid. *Dangerous Assets must either be left outside of the partnership or must be placed in one or more separate partnerships.* Dangerous Assets must be isolated from each other and from Safe Assets, in order to avoid contaminating the Safe Assets.

Dangerous Assets

Apartment buildings may be considered to be Dangerous Assets. The liability potential of apartment houses is particularly high. Although liability insurance coverage is usually available, the amount of coverage may not be sufficient. A fire in a densely populated building may cause severe injury or death to many tenants. The potential liability for such a tragedy could easily reach into the millions of dollars, exceeding by far the amount of your insurance coverage.

Apartment owners can also be held responsible for the acts of the resident managers. If the resident manager engages in race or sex discrimination in renting to tenants, or is guilty of sexual harassment, this liability may be imputed to you as the owner of the property. Acts such as these may not be covered under your standard insurance coverage.

If this asset is transferred to the same Family Limited Partnership which holds all of your other assets, that partnership, as the owner of the property would face a high degree of lawsuit exposure and all of your assets would again be at risk.

Instead, the best approach for a Dangerous Asset such as an apartment building would be to transfer that property to its own *separate* partnership. If a number of these type of properties were owned, each could be placed in a separate entity. Once we formed 19 different partnerships for a client, each holding one apartment building. If a disaster occurred, only the partnership which owned that property would be sued. The other properties and family assets would be safely insulated and shielded from liability under this arrangement.

Some types of commercial real estate may also constitute Dangerous Assets. Office buildings, hotels, restaurants, night clubs or any other building where many people work or gather, all have the potential to produce stratospheric liability in the event of some type of disaster. These properties must be kept separate from other types of assets.

Safe Assets

Safe Assets, with a low probability of creating lawsuit liability can be maintained in a single partnership.

Family Home

For most people the family home is their single most valuable asset. Fortunately, a house is a good candidate for asset protection in a Family Limited Partnership. It is unlikely that a house would create a substantial uninsured liability. Homeowners insurance provides protection against liability associated with ownership of the home and if someone is injured on the property, the amount of coverage should be sufficient to satisfy any claim.

The house can be transferred to the partnership by use of a simple quitclaim deed. Endorsements reflecting the new ownership should be secured from the liability and casualty insurer and the title insurance company.

Local law must be consulted in order to avoid triggering a property tax reassessment of the home. Some states, such as California, do not increase taxes on the assessed value of property unless there has been a change of ownership. But even if there is a change of ownership, property transferred from individuals to an entity controlled by those individuals is usually exempt from reassessment. Your own state law must be reviewed in order to understand the property tax implications of a transfer.

In addition to preparing a quitclaim deed to transfer the house, you may wish to obtain the consent of lender. If you have a loan on your home, the terms of the loan usually contain what is known as a "Due on Sale" clause. The Due on Sale clause states that the lender has the right to declare the loan due and payable if the property is transferred to another person or entity.

This is not quite as ominous as it sounds. The law in most states provides that a lender cannot exercise the Due on Sale clause, unless the security for the loan has been jeopardized by the transfer. If, for example, the property is transferred to a less creditworthy buyer, the lender may argue that its security has been impaired by the transaction. A transfer to a partnership, in which the borrowers on the loan are the general partners, should not be viewed as impairing the lenders security since the same persons as before are responsible for making the monthly payments. All the same, depending upon the law of your state, at least discussing the matter with your lender, prior to the transfer, may be the prudent course of action.

A tax issue which arises with respect to the transfer of the family home into the Family Limited Partnership concerns the availability of the income tax deduction for home mortgage interest. Section 163 of the Internal Revenue Code permits a deduction for "qualified residence interest." A "qualified residence" is defined as the "principal residence" of the taxpayer. The only requirements appear to be that (1) the house is the principal residence of the taxpayer; (2) interest is paid by the taxpayer; and (3) the taxpayer has a beneficial interest in any entity which holds legal title to the property. Based upon the language of the statute, the deduction for mortgage interest would, therefore, not seem to be adversely affected by a transfer into the Family Limited Partnership. However since the outcome of this issue obviously has great significance to you, you will need to discuss this with your personal tax advisor in order to reach a firm conclusion on this matter.

Similar tax issues concern the ability to rollover the gain from the sale of your home and the one time exclusion of gain available for individuals over age fifty-five. In order to avoid the possible loss of these benefits it appears that mere *legal title* could be transferred to the partnership while maintaining the beneficial ownership within the Asset Protection Trust. This arrangement would preserve all of the tax benefits while accomplishing the desired level of asset protection.

Bank and Brokerage Accounts

These type of accounts do not create any potential liability and should be transferred into the Family Limited Partnership. In order to open these accounts in the name of the partnership, you will present the financial institution with a certified copy of the Certificate of Limited Partnership. The institution will also require the Employer Identification Number issued to the partnership by the Internal Revenue Service.

Interest In Other Entities

The Family Limited Partnership is an excellent vehicle for holding interests in other business entities. The reason that we mention these other business entities is that the Family Limited Partnership must not ever be engaged in any business activities. You do not want the partnership to buy or sell property or goods or to enter into contracts. If the partnership does business then the partnership can get sued. And if the partnership gets sued and loses, all of the assets that it holds can be lost.

For example, a client of ours entered into a contract to purchase a shopping center. Previously, we had set up for him a Family Limited Partnership. Without our knowledge, the "Buyer" under the purchase contract was the Family Limited Partnership. During the pre-closing escrow period, financing became unavailable and the client failed to complete the deal. The seller sued the partnership for damages for breach of contract and was awarded $600,000 wiping out a substantial portion of our clients assets. The seller sued the partnership because the partnership was the named party to the contract.

This transaction should not have been handled in this manner. The proper way to conduct this type of business activity is through a separate corporate or partnership arrangement.

By using the proper planning techniques potential liability can be significantly reduced and valuable personal assets may be protected from a dangerous lawsuit. Had this arrangement been used, our client would not have lost $600,000. Instead, the buyer and seller would probably have re-negotiated the terms of the purchase in a way that was mutually satisfactory to each side.

This example illustrates the necessity for conducting business activities through an entity outside of the Family Limited Partnership so that family assets are not exposed to the risk of liability. The proper role of the Family Limited Partnership in this context is to hold the interests in the business entities that are themselves subject to risk.

The reason for this should now be apparent. If you own the shares of a corporation and you are sued, a successful creditor will seize the shares. He can then dissolve the corporation and reach its assets. Therefore, you would want to protect the corporate shares by placing them in the Family Limited Partnership.

The only potential drawback to the partnership owning the stock is that a partnership cannot be a shareholder of an S Corporation. Only individuals and certain types of trusts (e.g. grantor trusts) are permitted shareholders of this kind of stock. As a result, if the corporation has assets and you wish to hold the stock in the Family Limited Partnership, you cannot use an S Corporation. Alternatively, if you do not wish to use a C Corporation, an Asset Protection Trust, which qualifies as a grantor trust would provide the necessary protection of the corporate shares.

USING ASSET PROTECTION TRUSTS

THE ULTIMATE ASSET PROTECTION

In this Chapter we will show you that Asset Protection Trusts can be simple, straightforward and convenient to use and maintain, and that these trusts can produce the highest level of asset protection.

WHAT IS AN ASSET PROTECTION TRUST

In many ways an Asset Protection Trust looks exactly like a standard domestic trust. The settlor is the person who transfers the assets to the trust. The settlor is usually one of the trustees, together with a trust company, whose business is operated outside of the United States. In a typical trust, the trustees are given discretion to accumulate or distribute income among a specified class of beneficiaries. The settlor may be one the named beneficiaries, together with his spouse, children or grandchildren. One unique feature of this kind of a trust is the role of the "Protector". The Protector is a person, usually the settlor, whose consent is necessary for any activity to be conducted by the trustees. The term of the trust may be limited to a period of years or it may continue after the settlor's death.

WHAT PURPOSE DOES THE ASSET PROTECTION TRUST SERVE ?

One way to use a trust like this is to transfer cash, securities, or other liquid assets to an account established under the name of the trust at a bank of your choice in a foreign jurisdiction. The Protector then advises the trustees on the manner in which the funds are to be held or invested.

For those who are reluctant to transfer funds out of the United States until it is absolutely necessary to do so, the Family Limited Partnership can be used in conjunction with the Asset Protection Trust. Under this arrangement, Husband and Wife will be general partners with complete management and control over the partnership assets. Only the limited partnership interests are transferred to the trust.

The trustee has no right to interfere in the management of the partnership. Complete control is maintained by Husband and Wife as general partners. Even though the trust holds the limited partnership interests, *all of the assets of the partnership remain physically located in the United States under the direct control and supervision of the general partners.* Note that all family assets are held by the partnership. The only asset held by the trust is a partnership interest.

TAX TREATMENT OF ASSET PROTECTION TRUSTS

One of the most appealing aspects of the Asset Protection Trust is that, properly structured, it produces absolutely no income tax benefits. The trust is simply ignored for tax purposes. All of the income is included on the tax return of the U.S. settlor of the trust. The trust is treated in the same manner as a revocable living trust.

We say that this treatment is appealing because it allows us to establish these trusts without interference or scrutiny by the I.R.S. In fact, since the trust does not provide a mechanism for deferring or avoiding U.S. taxes, the I.R.S. is utterly indifferent to the creation of the Asset Protection Trust arrangement. Depending on the way the trust is structured, there may be certain disclosure requirements provided by law, but these forms are neither burdensome nor likely to cause any difficulties.

ASSET PROTECTION FEATURES

Asset Protection Trust versus Domestic Trust

An Asset Protection Trust provides infinitely superior asset protection results than can be achieved with a domestic irrevocable trust. The Asset Protection Trust will always be established in a country with laws which are more favorable to asset protection objectives than the laws in the United States

For example, the laws in some countries provide for a statute of limitations on fraudulent conveyances which can be as short as one year and the standard of proof required for a fraudulent conveyance is the difficult " beyond a reasonable doubt " rather than the lesser civil standard of a "preponderance of the evidence." The courts in these countries will not enforce a judgment rendered in the United States, or an order of a U.S. Bankruptcy Court. To prosecute a claim against the trust the creditor would have to go to that country and retry the underlying case, an almost impossible requirement.

A further advantage of the Asset Protection Trust is that a greater degree of flexibility can be achieved in the way in which the trust is established. The settlor of the trust can serve as both trustee and beneficiary, and the trust will still be valid under local law. This allows the settlor to retain a substantially greater degree of control and enjoyment over trust assets then would be permitted under U.S law with a domestic trust.

Of equal importance, an Asset Protection Trust allows a great deal more practical flexibility than a domestic trust in protecting the assets of the partnership. When the partnership interests are held by an Asset Protection Trust, the option is always open to move the assets of the partnership into an account established in the foreign jurisdiction in order to achieve ultimate protection.

For example, all partnership assets would normally remain in the partnership account at a local bank. But in the event of an attack on the partnership by a creditor, claiming fraudulent conveyance or some other theory, the funds could be moved into the Asset Protection Trust account, pursuant to the trustees duties to preserve the assets of the trust for the beneficiaries. To reach those funds the creditor would have to commence an action in the foreign jurisdiction and would have to overcome apparently insurmountable obstacles under the law of that jurisdiction.

Assets transferred to an offshore trust account in this manner will remain under the joint control of the settlors and the foreign trustee. Typically these accounts are established with two signatures required for transactions. The settlors will be one of the signatories and the foreign trustee will be the second signatory. This arrangement effectively bars the foreign trustee from making any unauthorized withdrawals and should ease any concerns about possible loss of control to a third party trustee. Although our experience is that the reputable trust companies are honest, reliable and responsive, it is probably not advisable to set-up a plan that is dependent upon the honesty of *any* third party for its success. Therefore, the foreign trustee should never be the sole signatory on the account

For additional protection, the settlors (as Protectors of the trust) can retain the power to change trustees at any time. If for any reason (and we have never seen such circumstances occur) the trustee attempted to block the withdrawal of funds, the Protectors could replace the trust company with another offshore trustee.

This strategy of moving assets to the offshore trust account must be modified if family assets consist exclusively of real estate, While cash and securities and personal property can be transferred offshore, real estate cannot be moved. In a fraudulent conveyance action concerning real estate, a local court has the power to change the title to the property. So if the creditor is successful, the real estate will be lost. On the other hand, a useful approach is to mortgage, refinance or sell real estate in the partnership in order to produce cash which can be effectively protected in the offshore account. There are also sophisticated strategies known as equity reduction plans which can successfully convert real estate equity into a protected cash account, thereby removing the asset from local court jurisdiction.

It bears repeating at this point that *any* transfer of property, where a fraudulent conveyance issue could conceivably by raised, should only take place under the guidance and supervision of a qualified attorney. A fraudulent conveyance involves civil as well as a criminal penalties and only a competent attorney can properly advise you on a particular course of action.

Assets Are Protected

When we previously discussed the fraudulent conveyance law in Chapter Five, we saw that transfers of assets with an intent to defraud a creditor or which rendered the transferor insolvent, may be set aside by a court. The problem for the creditor under these circumstances, even if he successfully persuades a judge or a jury that the transfer was fraudulent, is that a U.S. Court has no capacity to exercise its authority over a foreign trustee. Simply stated, a foreign person or company with no presence or assets in the United States cannot be compelled to act by a U.S. Court. If a U.S. Court ordered a foreign trustee to return fraudulently conveyed assets, the foreign trustee, under a duty to preserve trust assets, would refuse to comply with the order.

If a foreign person or entity has assets in the United States, a U.S. Court can exercise leverage over the foreign person by threatening or attempting to seize those assets for failure to comply with the order of the court. For example, on occasion the U.S. Government seeks information about foreign bank deposits in matters concerning criminal tax evasion, drug charges or securities law violations. Because of its local secrecy laws, the foreign bank usually fails to comply with the Government's request for information. However, when the foreign bank has assets, such as deposits or branches in the United States, the Government may threaten to seize the assets if the bank does not comply with the court order. Generally, this threat is successful and the bank will reveal the sought-after information.

Precisely for this reason, most foreign based trust companies do not conduct business or have assets in the United States. Any foreign trustee which is selected must have no local business activity in order to avoid the financial leverage which might then be applied by a U.S. Court.

Since the creditor cannot obtain satisfaction from obtaining a U.S. Court order against a foreign trustee, the only method for compelling the trustee to act is to file a lawsuit in the jurisdiction in which the trustee is located. Whether or not the creditor can be successful in this forum will depend upon the particular laws in effect in that country.

Contempt Orders Against U.S. Debtor

Can you, a U.S. resident and a settlor of a Asset Protection Trust, be ordered by a court to return assets transferred to the offshore account? A judgment creditor would certainly like to obtain such an order from the local court and whether he can do so depends upon the terms of the trust.

Clearly, if you have the right to retrieve the assets, a judge will order you to do so. Judges back up these orders with the power to hold a person in contempt of court for refusing to comply. The sole issue then is your legal ability to return transferred property pursuant to a court order.

This issue is resolved, in a properly drafted trust, by not giving the settlor any such power to revoke the trust or re-acquire the assets without the consent of the trustee. Although the trustee typically will comply with the wishes of the settlor, the trust agreement requires the trustee is to disregard any communications issued by the settlor under *duress*. That is, if the settlor is ordered by a court to communicate with the trustee, the trustee is required by the terms of the trust to ignore such requests for action.

As a result of this structure, the settlor has no legal right to revoke the trust and re-acquire trust assets. A court cannot compel an action that a person has no power to perform and the foreign trustee will not respond to orders from a court outside of its jurisdiction. The conclusion is that the assets of the trust are protected and the settlor cannot be held in contempt for failing to achieve a return of the property.

WHERE TO SET UP THE ASSET PROTECTION TRUST

Selecting the proper jurisdiction for the Asset Protection Trust is a matter of critical importance. As a general rule the jurisdiction should have a well established trust law favorable to asset protection strategies. Further, it should be inconvenient or nearly impossible for a U.S. creditor to reach the assets of the trust by commencing an action in the country in the foreign country.

KEY FACTORS

The particular factors which are important are as follows:

Ease of Communications

Communication with the foreign trustee must be convenient. Fortunately, the use of the fax machine and improvements in telephone technology have made communication with even the most geographically remote locations a relatively simple procedure. Using only English speaking countries avoids language barriers which can cause delays or costly mistakes.

Experienced and Well Established Trustees

The country where the trust is established must provide a choice of responsible and experienced trust companies from which to select a trustee. The trust companies must be experienced in the area of asset protection and must understand the nature of their peculiar responsibilities.

No or Low Tax Jurisdiction

Income earned by the Asset Protection Trust must not be subject to taxation in that jurisdiction.

Strict Bank Secrecy Laws

The country must impose strict limitations on disclosure of information by local banking institution.

Favorable Trust Laws

Many foreign jurisdictions do not recognize the existence of trusts or severely restrict these arrangements. It is important that the law of the country allows the greatest degree flexibility in establishing the trust to meet asset protection objectives.

Stable Local Government

Political and economic stability is essential to the proper functioning of the trust. A country which may have its legal system or its financial institutions disrupted by unexpected forces should not be chosen.

Favorable Asset Protection Laws

The existence of laws designed to encourage the formation of trusts used for asset protection strategies is an essential factor. If a creditor elects to file a lawsuit in the foreign jurisdiction seeking to set aside the trust, the laws of that country must make it impractical for the creditor to obtain a successful result. A country which does not recognize judgments of U.S Courts or federal agencies is critical to the success of the plan.

Absence of Exchange or Currency Controls

The ability to move funds, if necessary, in and out of the jurisdiction without interference or restriction by local authorities is a requirement in selecting a location.

Confidentiality

The country which is chosen must allow for complete confidentiality of information concerning the settlor and the beneficiaries of the trust.

THE MOST FAVORABLE LAWS

Several of the countries which have some or all of the features mentioned above are the Bahamas, Barbados, Bermuda, the Cayman Islands, the Cook Islands, and Gibraltar.

The Bahamas

The Bahamas is one of the oldest and most established financial centers in the world. It has strict bank secrecy laws, no income tax and a modern and sophisticated telecommunications structure. The location in the Caribbean is convenient to the United States. There are a number of excellent trust companies located in the Bahamas and local law allows a satisfactory degree of flexibility in the creation of Asset Protection Trusts.

Bermuda

Bermuda is a group of English speaking islands located in the western Atlantic Ocean approximately 800 miles from New York City. Bermuda has a well developed modern trust law. The country has no income tax or other form of taxation for profits or capital gains. Some professional advisers have complained that the Bermuda trust companies are difficult to work with, but it is hard to say whether these are isolated incidents or whether it represents a pattern of conduct sufficient to cause one to avoid Bermuda for these types of purposes.

Barbados

Barbados is located in the eastern Caribbean and has made great progress over the past ten years in becoming one of the leading offshore financial centers. If certain conditions are met, there is no Barbados income tax. Perhaps alone among the Caribbean tax havens, Barbados has sought to maintain good relations with the United States, leading some observers to conclude that some elements of bank secrecy and confidentiality may be eroded within the near future.

The Cayman Islands

The Cayman Islands are a group of three islands conveniently located just one hour's flight from Miami. The main island is Grand Cayman which has developed into a major offshore financial center. The population is small and homogeneous and enjoys a high standard of living. The islands enjoy an exceptional degree of political and economic stability. The trust law of the Cayman Islands provides excellent asset protection features and numerous trust companies are experienced and well established. The Cayman Islands have strict bank secrecy provisions and no local income taxes. The islands are one of the most popular places for establishing Asset Protection Trusts.

The Cook Islands

The Cook Islands are a group of islands in the South Pacific. Between 1901 and 1965, the islands were part of New Zealand and then became fully self-governing under a written constitution. The Cook Islands has no income tax and has been developing rapidly in recent years as a major offshore financial center. Under the International Trust Amendment Act (1989), the Cook Islands legislature has adopted laws which are the most favorable asset protection laws in the world. The Cook Islands has a number of trust companies who are experienced and helpful in asset protection matters. The availability of banking institutions is more limited than in the Caribbean countries, but at least one highly regarded international bank is available for opening trust accounts. Communications with the country are excellent and there is a time difference of only two hours from the west coast. The remote geographical location is either a drawback or an advantage, depending upon whether it is you or your creditor who is required to travel there.

Gibraltar

Gibraltar is a British territory located off the coast of Spain of the western entrance to the Mediterranean. Gibraltar is well known as a convenient international offshore haven and has many local professionals and trust companies of high quality and reputation. Foreign trusts are not subject to any taxes in Gibraltar. The trust laws contain some favorable asset protection features. Asset Protection Trusts established in Gibraltar by Amendments to the Bankruptcy Ordinance are registered with the local government. Although access to this special register is limited to the local government, some practitioners are concerned that confidentiality may be impaired by this requirement.

SUMMARY

Asset Protection Trusts are excellent devices for achieving a very significant level of asset protection. When used in conjunction with the Family Limited Partnership , assets remain in the United States under the exclusive control of the general partners. Asset Protection Trusts provide an advantage over domestic irrevocable trusts because the laws of the offshore jurisdiction will be more favorable than local U.S law and because the assets of an Asset Protection Trust will be difficult or impossible to retrieve by a judgment creditor. The proper jurisdiction for the trust must be carefully evaluated based upon the factors enumerated in this Chapter.

FIVE STEPS FOR COMPLETE ASSET PROTECTION

STEP ONE
REDUCE YOUR LAWSUIT EXPOSURE

You should make sure that you conduct your financial affairs in a manner which will minimize your exposure to lawsuits. There are plenty of real dangers out there which you cannot control. But some of the most troublesome sources of liability can be significantly reduced through sound business planning.

Avoid Business Partnerships

You should never enter into a business partnership with anyone. These types of partnerships can produce huge liabilities for you which are totally unexpected and not your fault. As a co-general partner you are responsible for all partnership debts and any negligent acts of your partners. A business partnership *expands* the scope of your personal liability when you should be trying to limit your risks.

Use a Corporation to do Business

A corporation can insulate you from many types of business risks and effectively diminishes your degree of personal liability. When you use a corporation you will not be responsible for a corporate obligation unless you have given your personal guarantee. You will be shielded from most types of claims from employees, suppliers and customers as well as from any injuries caused by your co-owners negligent acts.

Since a corporation is a taxpaying entity, you will have to have a plan for eliminating a potential double tax on corporate earnings. This can be accomplished by using an S Corporation or by zeroing out corporate income through salaries to officers.

In order to insure that the corporation will be respected for legal and tax purposes, the corporate formalities of minutes, bylaws and stock certificates must be observed. All of your dealings with third parties should be conducted in the corporate name and a separate corporate bank account must be used.

Never Give a Personal Guarantee

Much of the protection which can be accomplished with a corporation will be lost if you give a personal guarantee of a corporate obligation. Many of the problems which we see in our practice are caused directly by needless guarantees for corporate loans and leases for business ventures which were not successful.

We have found, in our practice, that a lender or a lessor will generally not require a personal guarantee if he can be persuaded that the business or proposed venture is sound. These days, lenders are anxious to make good loans and lessors want to lease empty space. If you cannot convince them that your company is going to be successful and that they should rely solely on the business for payment, you should not do the deal with them.

If you get turned down too many times, perhaps you are not being realistic about your prospects for success. Maybe your business plan is not really as good as you think. If you sign a personal guarantee you are placing all of your assets at the mercy of a particular business deal and you are undertaking a risk with odds much worse than those offered in most gambling casinos.

Use Multiple Entities

Those who have more than one type of business should use different entities to conduct each facet of the business. The goal is to insulate each separate business from liabilities produced by the other activities. If you own several real estate properties use different entities to hold each one. If there is a lawsuit in connection with one of the properties, the others won't be endangered. The same logic would be applied if you owned properties and also performed property management services for others. You would want to separate the management business from the ownership of the properties.

As a general principle, the ownership of Dangerous Assets, those with a high risk of producing liability, should always be separated from Safe Assets, such as cash or securities. These Safe Assets should not be jeopardized by a liability associated with your business or other Dangerous Assets which you own. For example, a client of ours owned a restaurant and had substantial retirement savings in the bank. If he was sued because of a liability in connection with the restaurant, his retirement savings could be lost. Instead, merely by incorporating the restaurant, we removed the Dangerous Asset from his legal ownership. Then, any lawsuit against the corporation which owned the business would not place his other assets at risk.

STEP TWO
PROTECT ASSETS WITH A
FAMILY LIMITED PARTNERSHIP

A Family Limited Partnership will provide you with four significant advantages which cannot be obtained through any other vehicle.

Discourages Lawsuit

Assets which are protected in the Family Limited Partnership cannot be seized by a judgment creditor. It is unlikely that someone will want to sue you if they do not believe that they will be able to collect a judgment.

Saves Income Taxes

As tax rates increase under the recent legislation, overall family income taxes may be reduced by shifting income to lower bracket family members. This can be accomplished by gifting some limited partnership interests to children or grandchildren who are fourteen years or older. Depending upon the number of beneficiaries and the amounts involved, over a period of years the total savings can be quite substantial.

Saves Estate Taxes

Limited Partnership interests which are transferred by gift to children or other family members, will not be included in your estate for estate tax purposes. A small percentage could be transferred each year which would not be subject to gift tax under the annual exclusion of $10,000 per donee. Further, the value of the interests transferred should be discounted in value to account for the lack of marketability and control. Very significant estate tax savings can be generated in this manner.

Protection of Assets

The most valuable feature of the Family Limited Partnership is the ability to protect and shield assets from potential claims. The law is well established that a creditor of a partner is not permitted to seize assets of the partnership to satisfy the debt. That means that the family home, savings and investments can be safely insulated from potential liabilities in this manner. The Family Limited Partnership is the proper method for owning and holding valuable assets for anyone who has any possible lawsuit or liability exposure.

STEP THREE
USE AN ASSET PROTECTION TRUST

The highest level of asset protection can be accomplished when an Asset Protection Trust (APT) is used to hold the limited partnership interests in the Family Limited Partnership. An APT has the following benefits:

Favorable Laws

An APT is designed to take advantage of the laws which are most favorable to asset protection objectives. In some jurisdictions there is a statute of limitations on fraudulent conveyances which is as short as one year. Laws which do not permit enforcement of U.S. judgments and Bankruptcy Court decrees present a substantial obstacle for your opponent to overcome.

Greater Legal Flexibility

The APT can be structured with far greater flexibility then a domestic trust. With an APT the settlor can be a co-trustee and a beneficiary and the trust will still be valid. The settlor can also retain very significant powers over the trust without jeopardizing its asset protection features.

Greater Practical Flexibility

When the APT is combined with the Family Limited Partnership control and management of the assets is retained by you as the general partner of the Family Limited Partnership. However, if there is ever a legal threat which might endanger the assets of the partnership, liquid assets would be moved into the APT account for protection. Other assets could be sold or refinanced in order to produce cash which can be preserved in the APT account. Assets in the APT account, outside of the jurisdiction of a U.S. Court, would provide a virtually insurmountable barrier to recovery.

STEP FOUR
MAKE ESTATE PLANNING DECISIONS

All of your major estate planning objectives can be accomplished with the Family Limited Partnership and the Asset Protection Trust.

Avoiding Probate

Probate is an inconvenient, expensive and time consuming process. It exposes private family matters and financial affairs to public scrutiny. The APT insures that your assets are not subject to probate proceedings and provides for continuity of management of family assets.

Reducing or Eliminating Estate Taxes

The overall plan provides a mechanism for reducing or eliminating federal estate taxes by creating a vehicle for you to make annual gifts of limited partnership interests, if you so desire. The APT also contains provisions to minimize estate taxes by dividing into the A and B trusts as previously discussed. This arrangement will allow up to $1,200,000, under current law, to pass to your children free of estate taxes.

Leaving Your Property to Whom You Choose

The APT insures that your property will be left to those persons you choose in the manner you wish. You can establish the rules regarding the distribution of income and principal for your ultimate beneficiaries. At any time during your life you have the power to add or remove beneficiaries according to your personal wishes.

STEP FIVE
GET COMPETENT
PROFESSIONAL ADVICE

Designing your overall asset protection plan and preparing the documents necessary for the Family Limited Partnership and Asset Protection Trust must take place under the guidance and supervision of an attorney who specializes in these matters. Although the number of qualified attorneys has been limited in the past, a growing number throughout the country are developing the necessary expertise.

Legal fees for creating the Family Limited Partnership, the Asset Protection Trust and the offshore APT bank account will vary considerably depending upon the complexity of your financial affairs. For those clients who know what they want and require a minimum amount of attorney time, it is possible to prepare all of the necessary documentation for fees which are substantially reduced. If you need assistance in finding an attorney in your area or would like to discuss your personal situation please feel free to call our offices at (800) 223-4291.

THE LIMITED LIABILITY COMPANY

A new development which is gaining popularity in many states is the entity known as the Limited Liability Company (LLC). The LLC was first adopted in Wyoming and Florida and a total of forty-six states now allow the LLC. California is the most recent state to enact this legislation.

The purpose of the LLC is to provide business owners with the very favorable liability protection of corporations coupled with the informality and tax advantages available from partnerships.

An LLC is generally formed by a central filing with the Secretary of State. Unlike corporations, ownership is not evidenced by share certificates, but rather by an entry in the company books. Instead of corporate minutes and bylaws, the operation of the business is controlled through an Operating Agreement which is similar to a partnership agreement.

The LLC is a pass-through entity, like a partnership. The taxable income or loss is reported on the tax returns of the owners. This avoids the potential for double taxation which exists with a corporation. Although this same tax result can generally be achieved with an S Corporation, the LLC is not subject to many of the restrictions that apply to S Corporations. For example, the requirements that the S Corporation have no more than thirty-five shareholders; only one class of stock; and that the shares can only be held by a natural person or some types of trusts, do not apply to the LLC.

Any person or other entity is permitted as a member of the LLC. However, as with a partnership, there must be two or more individuals or legal entities involved. For instance, the members of the LLC can be composed of two corporations, an individual and a corporation, two trusts, a partnership and a trust, or any other permutation which can be imagined. Because of the degree of freedom which is permitted, many new and favorable strategies for business and personal financial planning can be achieved.

The LLC can also be administered and maintained without the rigid requirements which apply to corporations. The LLC has no formal hierarchy of directors and officers. The owners of the business are substantially free to manage the company and divide the profits and the ownership in any manner they choose.

The LLC also represents a significant improvement over the partnership as an entity for doing business or holding assets. As we have discussed, doing business in partnership form exposes each of the partners to personal liability for all obligations of the partnership. Even with a limited partnership, there is still a general partner with unlimited liability for all of the debts of the partnership.

In contrast, the LLC protects *all* of the owners of the business from liabilities associated with the company. None of the owners are personally responsible for any debts or claims against the business.

As with a partnership, a creditor of a member of

an LLC is not permitted to reach the assets of the LLC. Instead, the creditor is allowed to obtain a charging order against the members interest in the LLC. Perhaps, the law will allow a foreclosure of such an interest, under the same logic as applied in the *Hellman* case previously discussed. But in either event it is clear that a creditor with a charging order or foreclosure would not become a member of the LLC and would not be entitled to vote or participate in management.

California has placed some limitations on the use of LLC's which must be considered. Professionals, such as a doctors and lawyers, are not permitted to use an LLC to conduct their practice. Also, the state imposes a surtax on an LLC beginning at gross revenues of $250,000. The amount of the surtax starts at $500 and can increase to as much as $4,500 for LLC's with gross income of $5,000,000 or more. This fact will be a consideration in determining whether an active business, producing significant revenues, should be structured as an LLC.

STRATEGIES FOR USING THE LLC

The LLC represents a very effective business planning tool in a wide variety of circumstances:

The LLC is an excellent alternative to a corporation to conduct your active business. The threat of double taxation is avoided and considerable flexibility and convenience can be achieved. Because the corporate formalities of minutes, bylaws, officers, directors, meetings etc. have been eliminated, it appears that a creditor of the LLC will not have the ability to "pierce the corporate veil" and establish personal liability on the part of a member of the LLC. In this manner the LLC adds a level of security and certainty which exceeds that available from a corporation. In states, such as California, which impose a surtax on gross revenues, the disadvantage of the additional cost must be considered.

For asset protection and estate planning purposes, an LLC can be used as the General Partner of a Family Limited Partnership. Instead of Husband and Wife serving as General Partners, as in our usual case, an LLC composed of Husband and Wife would be the General Partner of the Family Limited Partnership. This technique would allow you to obtain the benefits of the Family Limited Partnership without exposing either Husband or Wife, as individual General Partners, to the threat of lawsuits and the risk of personal liability for partnership debts.

The LLC is the best means of holding joint interests in real estate. If you own property with someone else as a joint tenant, tenant in common or in a partnership, you have individual liability for any claims against the property or the partnership. In addition, your interest in the property can be lost or jeopardized if your co-owner incurs any obligations. Instead, if property is held in an LLC, a claim against you, the company or your co-owner will not affect the property.

The LLC represents an exciting and powerful new form of business organization with advantages that cannot be achieved through any of the traditional arrangements. Although all of the technical ramifications have not yet been settled, the LLC should be given serious consideration for business, estate planning and asset protection strategies.

DETAILED DISCUSSION

INCOME TAX EFFECT OF A CHARGING ORDER

A creditor who obtains a charging order runs the risk of being taxed on income of the partnership, even though such income is not distributed. For example, a partnership owns an apartment building with a tax basis of $100,000. It sells the building for $1,000,000 in 1993. The partnership has a taxable gain of $900,000. Since the partnership is not itself a taxpaying entity, the taxable gain is allocated among the partners according to their respective ownership percentages. The partners receive this allocation of income regardless of whether the partnership actually distributes any cash.

There is some authority for the position that a creditor with a charging order is treated as a partner for purposes of receiving allocations of partnership income or loss. *Revenue Ruling 77-137*, 1977-1 CB 178. Under the facts which we have posed, a creditor with a charging order against a 50% partnership interest, for a judgment of $100,000, would have taxable income from the partnership of $450,000. Again, this is so even though the partnership holds onto the proceeds from the sale and nothing is distributed to the creditor or the other partners. Since the creditor will have to pay a tax liability of over $200,000 in attempting to collect a judgment of $100,000, the charging order would be a very unsatisfactory method of collecting this debt. The same result would be reached if the creditor obtained a foreclosure on the debtor's partnership interests rather then a charging order.

CROCKER AND HELLMAN

The citations for the *Crocker* and *Hellman* cases are as follows: *Crocker National Bank v. Perreton,* 208 Cal.App.3d 1, 255 Cal.Rptr.794 (1989): *Hellman v. Anderson,* 233 Cal.App. 3d 840, 284 Cal. Rptr. 830 (1991)

CREDITORS ABILITY TO REACH ASSETS OF DOMESTIC TRUST

The general rule is that an interest in a trust is reachable by the creditors of a settlor if the settlor has retained (1) a power to revoke the trust; (2) certain beneficial interests in the trust; (3) such unbridled control over the trust that no valid trust is deemed to exist.

1. California Probate Code Section 18200
This section states that if the settlor of a trust retains the power to revoke the trust in whole or in part, the trust property is subject to the claims of creditors of the settlor to the extent of the power of revocation during the lifetime of the settlor. An example of a trust which is revocable in this manner is the popular living trust which is commonly used as estate planning tool. Since the terms of that type of trust provide that the trust may be revoked during the lifetime of the settlor,

198

it is clear that under California law and under the general rule, the assets of such a trust would be reachable by any creditor of the settlor.

2. California Probate Code Section 15304

California Probate Code Section 15304(a) states that if the settlor is a beneficiary of a trust created by the settlor and the settlor's interest is subject to a provision restraining the voluntary or involuntary transfer of the settlor's interest, the restraint is invalid against the creditors of the settlor.

California Probate Code Section 15304(b) provides that if the settlor is the beneficiary of a trust created by the settlor and the trust instrument provides that the trustee shall pay income or principal or both for the support or education of the beneficiary or gives the trustee discretion to determine the amount of income or principal or both to be paid for the benefit of the settlor, a creditor of the settlor may reach the maximum amount that the trustee could pay to or for the benefit of the settlor under the terms of the trust instrument, not exceeding the amount of the settlors proportionate contributions to the trust.

Taken together, these California statutes establish the general rule that **if a settlor is also the beneficiary of the trust, the assets of the trust will not be shielded from the creditors of the settlor.** This rule applies if the settlor is an income beneficiary or if the trustee has discretion to distribute income or principal to the settlor. This is a codification of the well established principle that "(o)ne cannot, by any disposition of his own property, put the same or the income thereof beyond the reach of his creditors, so long as he himself retains the right to receive and use it." *McColgen v. Magee,* 155 P. 995. Section 156 of the Restatement Second of Trusts (1957) upholds the principles set forth in the California statutes.

3. Invalid Trust

The third circumstance under which trust assets might be reachable by a creditor of a settlor is when the trust itself is invalid because of the extent of the powers retained by the settlor. The general rule is that the trust is valid and remains intact even if the settlor is the trustee and retains extensive control over trust assets. *Oken v. Hammer* 791 P.2d 9: *Roberts v. South Oklahoma City Hospital Trust* 742 P.2d 1077 However, if the settlor retains "unbridled" control over the property, notwithstanding the existence of a named beneficiary, there is no valid trust and the creditors of the settlor can reach the assets of the trust. *Cleveland Trust Co. v. White,* 15 N.E 2d 627; *Halliburton Co. v. E.H. Owen Family Trust,* 773 S.W.2d 453; See also, e.g. *Matter of Estate of Kovalyshyn,* 343 A.2d 852 (N.J. 1975): *Johnson v. Commercial Bank,* 588 P.2d 1096 (Ore., 1978); *Restatement (Second) of Trusts,* Section 156 (1957)

Income Taxation of Grantor Trusts

Sections 671-678 of the Internal Revenue Code treat the settlor of a trust as the owner of trust property for income tax purposes if the settlor retains certain enumerated powers over the trust. If the settlor is so treated as the owner of trust property, all items of income and loss are reported directly on settlors individual tax return and the trust is ignored for federal income tax purposes. Such trusts are referred to for tax purposes as "grantor trusts."

For example, Section 674 of the Internal Revenue Code states that the settlor is treated as the owner of a trust in which he retains a power to control the beneficial enjoyment of the corpus or the income, subject to certain limited exceptions.

With a domestic trust or an Asset Protection Trust the settlor will usually retain the power to change the interests of the trust beneficiaries. This power comes within Section 674. As a result, a domestic or Asset Protection Trust over which the settlor has retained this power will be treated as a grantor trust and the income and loss will be reportable directly on the federal tax return of the settlor.

Attorney's Liability

If an attorney aides a client in a scheme to defraud creditors the attorney is committing a crime and is subject to disciplinary action by the state bar. *Yokozeki v. State Bar* 11 C3d 436, 521 P.2d 858 (1974), cert. denied 95 S.Ct 183, 419 US 900; see also *Allen v. State Bar*, 20 C3d 172, 141 Cal. Rptr. 808 (1977).

Future vs. Possible Creditors

The fraudulent conveyance law in most states applies to "future" as well as present creditors. The class of "future" creditors does not apply to anyone who may become a creditor at some later date. Instead the cases make it clear that the term refers to persons whom the transferor intended to defraud at the time of the transfer. For example if an individual transferred his property to another for protection purposes prior to engaging in a scheme to defraud others, the victims of the fraud would probably be covered under the class of "future" creditors. However, absent such a scheme to defraud, protections of one's assets from unknown claimants would not be considered to be a fraudulent conveyance. *Wantulok et. al. v. Wantulok* 214 P.2d 477 (Wyo. 1950)

Of particular interest is the case involving a physician who took various steps to insulate his assets after he lost his malpractice liability insurance. He was involved in an act of malpractice the following year and was subsequently sued by the patient. In an action to set aside the previous asset transfers the court distinguished between "probable" and "possible" future creditors. The trial court found that the plaintiff in the case was only a "possible" future creditor who was not intended to be protected under the fraudulent conveyance statute. The case was remanded on appeal to determine whether the doctor harbored an actual fraudulent intent at the time the assets were transferred. *Hurlbert v. Shackleton,* 560 S.2d 1276 (Fla. 1989).

Contempt Orders Against A U.S. Settlor

Under the usual Asset Protection Trust agreement the settlor will be a co-signatory on the account which is established outside of the United States. This account will require the signature of the settlor (as co-trustee) *and* the trust company. If a U.S. judge were to order the settlor to return the funds the settlor would be unable to comply, without the signature of the trust company. Since the trust company would be prohibited under the trust agreement from complying with orders of a U.S judge or a settlor under duress, the settlor would not have the legal capacity to obtain a return of the funds under these circumstances. The settlor should not be held in contempt of court for failing to perform an act which he is legally unable to accomplish. See e.g. *Bryan*, 339 U.S. 323 (S.Ct., 1950); *Healy*, 186 F.2d 164 (CA-9, 1950). A party cannot claim impossibility of performance if he himself has created the impossibility. *American Fletcher Mortgage Co. Inc. v. Bass,* 688 F.2d 513 (CA-7, 1982). However, there must be a connection between the order and the creation of the impossibility. See e.g. *F.T.C. v. Blaine*, 308 F.Supp, 932 (DC Ga., 1970). In a properly and timely drafted trust arrangement it does not appear that the necessary connection would be deemed to exist.

Section 1491 Excise Tax

Internal Revenue Code Section 1491 imposes an excise tax equal to 35% of the unrecognized gain on transfers to a Asset Protection Trust. However, relief is provided by Revenue Ruling 87-61 which holds that the excise tax is inapplicable if the grantor is treated as the owner of trust property under the provisions of Sections 671-678 of the Code. Under almost all circumstances the grantor will be so treated and the 35% excise tax will not be applied.

Domestic vs. Foreign Trust Classification

A trust which is established under the laws of a foreign country may be classified as either a foreign or a domestic trust for U.S. tax purposes. The proper characterization has great significance since foreign trusts have certain filing and disclosure requirements which do not pertain to domestic trusts. The issue of classification is determined based upon the following factors:

- The country where the trust is established

- The situs of trust assets

- The nationality and residence of the trustees

- The nationality and residence of the beneficiaries

- The nationality and residence of the settlor; and

- The situs of trust administration

Usually it will be desirable to have the Asset Protection Trust treated as a domestic trust for tax purposes in order to avoid the inconvenience of the various filing requirements. It is fairly easy to draft the trust so that the weight of the above factors leans most heavily on the side of classification as a domestic trust.

Choosing The Appropriate Offshore Jurisdiction

There are a number of factors to consider in selecting the proper jurisdiction in which to establish the offshore trust.

- The standard applied in determining what constitutes a fraudulent conveyance

- The burden of proof required to establish a fraudulent conveyance
- The Statute of Limitations for fraudulent conveyances
- Whether a finding of a fraudulent conveyance voids the trust or only the fraudulent conveyance of property
- Whether a settlors subsequent bankruptcy or insolvency renders a trust void or voidable
- Whether foreign judgments will be enforced in the trust jurisdiction
- The treatment of the common law perpetuity period
- How the law deals with U.S. property interests such as community property
- Does the law permit the settlor to retain a beneficial interest in the trust
- The applicability of forced heirship rights
- Whether "spendthrift" provisions restricting creditors access to beneficial interests are valid in the jurisdiction
- Does the law permit a transfer of situs to the jurisdiction of a trust created elsewhere
- The extent to which the law protects the confidentiality of the trust agreement, the settlors and the beneficiaries
- The existence of treaties or agreements between the trust jurisdiction and other countries

- The effect of an order by a bankruptcy court in the settlor's home country, and

- The degree to which the law of the trust situs is certain, settled and unambiguous

The manner in which a jurisdiction resolves or fails to resolve these issues will determine whether that country is a favorable candidate in which to establish a trust for asset protection.

The Trust Law Of The Cook Islands

The most significant issues have been successfully addressed by the trust law in the Cook Islands. The Cook Islands are a group of islands in the South Pacific, located south of Hawaii and north of New Zealand. Its closest neighbors are Tahiti and Samoa. Until 1965 the country was a Protectorate of New Zealand but it now has its own parliamentary government. The population of the country is about 18,000, most of whom live on the island of Rarotonga.

In 1989 and 1991 the International Trusts Act (ITA) was amended to create a clear and comprehensive statutory scheme for asset protection trusts, free of the substantial uncertainty and confusion which exists in the law of most other jurisdictions. Some of the key provisions of the ITA are as follows;

- The law allows for the establishment of an International Trust (IT) whose settlor and beneficiary are non-residents of the Cooks

- An IT will not be void in the event of the bankruptcy or insolvency of the settlor

- For purposes of fraudulent conveyances, the solvency of the settlor is determined with reference to the fair market value of the settlors remaining property after the transfer. If the fair market value of the remaining property exceeded the value of the creditors claim at that time, a fraudulent intent is conclusively absent

- The Statute of Limitations for a fraudulent conveyance action is the longer of two years from the date the creditors cause of action accrued or one year from the date of the transfer to the trust. All actions are barred two years from the date of the transfer to the trust

- A trust is not invalid because the settlor retains the rights to revoke or amend the trust or remove and appoint a new trustee. Further, it is permissible for the settlor to be a beneficiary of the trust, either alone or in conjunction with others

- A foreign judgment or decree of bankruptcy cannot be enforced against the trust, the settlor, trustee or protector

- The trust shall not be subject to any forced heirship provisions in the settlors home country

- A trust may contain a spendthrift provision restricting the alienation of a trust interest and the ability of a creditor to seize or attach the beneficiary's interest

- A term of the trust expressly selecting the law of the Cook Islands to govern the trust is valid, effective and conclusive regardless of any other circumstances

- The law protects the confidentiality of the trust by requiring registration of a certificate stating the name of the trust, but not the names of the settlor, the beneficiaries or the details of the trust agreement

Enforcement of U.S. Bankruptcy Decrees

A number of other countries have adopted asset protection laws which deal with some, but not all of the issues which have been resolved by the Cook Islands legislation. The Bahamas, Belize, Bermuda, British Virgin Islands, Cayman Islands, Gibraltar and Turks and Caicos all have favorable asset protection trust laws. The problem with these jurisdictions is that as members of the British Commonwealth they are required under Section 426 of the United Kingdom Insolvency Act of 1986 to grant reciprocal enforcement of U.K and Commonwealth bankruptcy decrees. If a United States bankruptcy decree is entered in the United Kingdom it appears that the decree would then be enforceable in the Commonwealth nations. Pending clarification of this issue the efficacy of the asset protection laws of these countries is subject to some question.

Due Diligence By The Trustees

By statute or internal practice a trust will not be accepted for registration in the "asset protection" jurisdictions without some degree of due diligence and satisfaction regarding the financial circumstances of the settlor.

An example of the most severe due diligence requirements is set forth in the Gibraltar Bankruptcy

(Register of Dispositions) Regulations 1990. It provides that before a trust can be registered the Trustees must make exhaustive inquiries concerning the settlor and must;

- Confirm that they have obtained an affidavit of solvency from the settlor

- Confirm that the settlor has completed forms of inquiry which details his current financial position

- Confirm that they have made all reasonable efforts to independently check the financial information given by the settlor; and

- Within twenty eight days of the anniversary of registration notify the Registrar of any changes in the initial information

Although Gibraltar may be among the most stringent with respect to information concerning the settlor's financial status, all jurisdictions will require some type of assurance of the settlor's solvency. The trust companies in the Cook Islands will generally not accept a trust for registration unless the trust is submitted by a U.S. attorney with whom the trust company is familiar and comfortable. The settlor will be required to provide details about any pending or threatened lawsuits and must represent that he will be solvent and able to meet his foreseeable obligations after the transfer to the trust.

Estate Planning Benefits Of The Asset Protection Trust

An Asset Protection Trust is a superior device for accomplishing a variety of financial and estate planning objectives.

- Avoiding probate and maintaining privacy concerning the settlor's assets and the disposition of his estate

- Minimizing or eliminating estate taxes through the use of the bypass trust format discussed previously

- Avoiding will contests and litigation arising out of disputes between family members

- Achieving the highest level of confidentiality and privacy concerning financial and business affairs

- Creating a flexible vehicle for international investment and asset management; and

- Protecting family wealth from claims and liabilities

Key Provisions Of The Asset Protection Trust

Trustees

One or more of the trustees will always be a trust company or other fiduciary domiciled in the jurisdiction selected to establish the trust. Usually the settlors of the trust will serve as co-trustees together with the trust company. The trustees are responsible for safeguarding and preserving trust assets for the benefit of the beneficiaries.

Discretionary Trust

The trust is structured as a "discretionary trust." This means that the trustees are not required to make regular distributions of income or principal. Instead, any such distributions are made only when the trustees deem it to be advisable.

The Protector

The settlors designate a person to act as the "Protector" of the trust. The consent of the Protector is necessary for the trustees to perform any act. Usually the settlors will serve as Protector. The Protector has the power to remove a trustee, at any time for any reason, and appoint a new trustee.

The Beneficiaries

The beneficiaries of the trust may be anyone initially designated by the settlors, including the settlors themselves. Beneficiaries may be added or removed by the trustees with the consent of the Protector.

Excluded Persons

Certain people, known as Excluded Persons, are prohibited from becoming a beneficiary, trustee or Protector of the trust. These Excluded Persons include creditors of the settlor or anyone appointed by a court. The purpose of this provision is to insure that no portion of the trust can be used to benefit anyone other than the beneficiaries of the trust.

Anti-Duress Clause

Under normal circumstances the trust company will comply with the wishes of the Protector. However, wishes which are expressed under order by a court cannot be followed by the trust company. This is known as the Anti-Duress Clause. For example, if a local court tried to reach assets of the trust by ordering the settlor to instruct the trust company to return funds to the United States, the trust company would not comply with such a request. Since the court has no jurisdiction over the trust company itself or the assets of the trust, the Anti-Duress Clause presents an enormous obstacle to recovery by a creditor.

Removal of Trust From Jurisdiction

Under circumstance where the trust or the beneficiaries are placed in danger or trust assets are subject to attack, the trust can be relocated to a different jurisdiction. For instance, even if a U.S. creditor filed a lawsuit in the Cook Islands, attempting to set aside a trust established there on the grounds of a fraudulent conveyance, the trust and its assets could be moved to another jurisdiction, such as the Cayman Islands. If the creditor followed, the trust would again be moved to the Isle of Man. The enormous cost and time involved in pursuing this moving target would certainly exhaust event the most determined and well financed opponent.

Assets of the Trust

In most cases, the assets of the trust will consist exclusively of partnership interests in the Family Limited Partnership. It is the Family Limited Partnership which actually holds any real estate and bank accounts. The reason for this is simply that most people prefer not to involve a third party (the trust company) in the ownership and management of their property. When only the partnership interests are held by the trust, individuals are able to maintain exclusive control and authority over their property while enjoying the significant protection afforded by the trust arrangement.

Offshore Bank Account

One or more accounts are usually established for the trust at selected offshore locations. The bank where the account is opened may or may not be in the same country as the trust company. For instance a trust could be established in Gibraltar but an account might be opened at a bank in Bermuda. The choice of banks will be limited to those in jurisdictions with strict bank secrecy laws. Since your deposits in these banks will not be insured, the financial strength of the bank will be most important. There are a number of very large, financially sound banks with branches in the Caribbean countries, Gibraltar, the Isle of Man and the Cook Islands.

The usual practice is to open the account with a minimal deposit. Many banks require a balance of at least $5,000, but others will permit an account with as little as $100. In most cases, only that minimal amount will ever be deposited in the offshore bank. All other funds remain in the partnership account in your local bank. If, at some point, there is a danger of a legal attack on the partnership, funds can then be wire transferred immediately from the local partnership account to the offshore trust account. For the reasons previously discussed, a creditor attempting to reach the assets of the trust would have to overcome substantial legal obstacles .

The terms of the offshore account can be designed in several ways. One option is to have the trust company act as the sole signatory on the account. Although we have never encountered an instance of dishonesty on the part of a reputable trust company over the course of many years of practice, we prefer not to create an arrangement that depends upon the honesty of any third party for the success of the plan. Instead, we prefer to design the structure so that funds in the account *cannot* be withdrawn without the signature of the settlor (in his capacity as co-trustee). This is accomplished through the use of a joint account, requiring the signature of *both* the settlor and the trust company. Although this would give the trust company the legal right to *block* a withdrawal of funds by the settlor, if this occurred the Protector would simply remove and replace the trust company. The trust company has no incentive to interfere with the Protector's wishes, except for those which would violate the express terms of the trust or their obligation to protect the interests of the beneficiaries. Again, in our experience and to the best of our knowledge, there has never been an instance in which one of the reputable trust companies has failed to be fully responsive and cooperative.

Asset Protection In Special Situations

Corporations and partnerships which carry on a business are especially vulnerable to lawsuits and claims. One of the primary objectives of asset protection is to restructure a company's financial affairs to minimize the risk of loss from unexpected claims.

Multiple Entities

Separate lines of business should be conducted through separate entities. In the real estate business it would be preferable to own each project in a different entity. The goal is to insulate each asset from the other so that a liability produced by one asset will not "contaminate" the others. One of our clients owned fifteen fast food hamburger franchises in a single corporation. If one of the franchises failed or a customer was injured—all of the stores would be jeopardized. The ideal approach was to separately incorporate each franchise

Patents and Copyrights

Companies which hold valuable patents or copyrights should attempt to reorganize the manner in which these assets are owned. For example, when a publishing company acquires a copyright from an author it should use a separate limited partnership or corporation as an intermediary. The acquiring entity (LP-1) would enter into the business deal with the author, receiving a copyright in exchange for a royalty contract. LP-1 would then license the copyright to the publishing company (PC). In the event of a judgment against PC, the creditor would not be able to reach the valuable copyrights, since they are owned by LP-1. The creditor would be able to reach the licenses which PC holds, but if the licenses were structured to last only for short terms, renewable by mutual agreement between PC and LP-1, the licenses would not have any value in the hands of a creditor. Despite the fact of a judgment, LP-1 would still be free to utilize the copyrights to continue producing income.

The same logic would also apply to the treatment of patents which are owned by a company. The objective is to remove valuable assets from the lawsuit vulnerable party by transferring the assets to an entity which is insulated from liability.

Accounts Receivable and Inventory

It is difficult to remove accounts receivable and inventory from a company's balance sheet without causing major problems from an accounting and tax standpoint. However, when these assets constitute a substantial portion of a company's net worth some form of protection is necessary.

One useful approach would be for the company to arrange bank financing equal to most of the value of the inventory and receivables This cash is then distributed to the owners of the business who contribute it to a Family Limited Partnership. The Partnership would pledge the cash to the bank as additional security for the loan. As the inventory is sold and receivables are collected the company receipts would be used to make payments on the loan. As the loan balance is reduced, the cash pledged by the Partnership would become available to the Partnership. The Partnership could then loan these funds to the company for working capital. As new inventory and receivables are acquired the cycle of bank financing and distributions would continue.

The result of this arrangement is that the value of the inventory and accounts receivable are always subject to a bank lien and the equity in these assets is effectively transferred from the company to the Family Limited Partnership. This technique will successfully shield the value of the inventory and receivables from claims against the company.

Machinery and Equipment

These assets can be financed in the same manner as the inventory and receivables. Alternatively, the assets themselves can be transferred to the owner of the company who then contributes them to a Family Limited Partnership. The Partnership would lease the machinery and equipment to the company in exchange for rental payments. This approach achieves several worthwhile objectives. (1) The assets are nicely protected in the Family Limited Partnership; (2) Surplus cash can be moved into a protected position in the FLP; and (3) Cash in the form of rental payments is not subject to payroll tax withholding and may, therefore, be less expensive than payments to the owner in the form of wages.

CASE STUDY

The best way to tie together the strategies we have discussed is to give you an example of one of our experiences with a client.

The Cautious Condominium Developer

Al was a successful real estate developer, enjoying the California real estate boom to its fullest in the late 1980's. He owned half a dozen apartment projects and a home in Beverly Hills worth $2 million. His net worth was close to $6 million.

In 1990 he came to our office and announced that he was going to build a $40 million condominium project on land that he owned in West Los Angeles. A local bank was willing to loan Al the entire $40 million to build the project. The bank wanted Al to personally guarantee the loan.

As all real estate developers must be, Al was very enthusiastic about the project. The market was great and he felt he was really going to make a killing on the deal. He asked our advice about creating a plan that would minimize the taxes on his anticipated profits.

After dealing with the tax issues, we gingerly asked if he had considered what would happen if things did not go quite as well as he expected. "What will happen if the market is bad when you're finished building. Are you prepared to lose everything on this deal?" We suggested that an asset protection plan should be created to protect his other properties and his home in case the deal didn't work out. Although Al felt that this was a waste of time and money, he agreed and we went forward with the plan.

We transferred all of Al's properties, including his home, to a Family Limited Partnership. Al and his wife were each 1% general partners. The other 98% of limited partnership interests were transferred to a newly created Asset Protection Trust formed in the Cook Islands. Al , his wife and his children were the beneficiaries of the trust. The trust was set up in a way so that there was no gift tax liability and Al maintained all of the income tax consequences connected with the properties. The actual development and ownership of the condominium project would be in the name of a corporation established for this purpose.

In order to finalize the loan, Al gave the lender his financial statement, which accurately revealed his interest in the Family Limited Partnership. The loan was made and he began to build the project.

By the time the project was completed, one year later, the condominium market has slowed dramatically. Prices for units were heading down. A year later, Al had sold only 26 of the 200 units. Eventually, the bank foreclosed on the project and told Al that he was responsible for the $12 million deficiency on the loan which he had personally guaranteed.

As the bank was getting ready to file a lawsuit against Al, we spoke to their attorney and told him that they would not be able to collect on any judgment they obtained. Under the law, the bank was prohibited from reaching the assets which had been transferred to the Family Limited Partnership. Also, since 98% of the limited partnership interests were owned by the trust, the bank would not be able to get a charging or a foreclosure against those partnership interests. We further pointed out that this arrangement had been created prior to the time the bank made the loan and Al had truthfully disclosed all of this information on his financial statement. Accordingly, there were no grounds to set aside the transfers as a fraudulent conveyance.

The lawyers for the bank knew that an action against Al would be futile and we agreed to a settlement of $150,000. Although Al's assets were solidly protected, we preferred not to have the bank obtain a judgment. Since a judgment can stand for as long as 20 years, we did not want to impair Al's ability to do business in the future. We felt that we had successfully protected Al's $6 million nest egg and that a settlement for $150,000 was a reasonable price to pay under the circumstances.

The plan was successful for three reasons: (1) The structure was created *before* Al got into trouble. If we had waited until later, there would have been a serious problem about the fraudulent conveyance issue. Since the amount of the deficiency was so large,-$12 million-the bank would have had every incentive to litigate the issue and probably would have been successful. It was clearly the early planning that saved the day; (2) Al fully disclosed to the bank in his loan application that all of his assets had been transferred to the Family Limited Partnership. That made it impossible for them to claim that Al has misled them or concealed information. There were simply no grounds to set aside the partnership arrangement; and (3) The plan was properly structured from a legal standpoint. The bank would not have been permitted to reach any of the assets in the partnership or the partnership interests held in the trust.

Negotiating With The Bank

A client of ours named Peter had a fairly typical problem. He owned an apartment building with a value of $1,000,000 encumbered by a loan of $900,000 which he had personally guaranteed to his bank. His other assets consisted primarily of about $200,000 of cash.

Peter was concerned that the bank would ask him to pay down a portion of the guaranteed debt with his available cash. He did not wish to do this since he wanted to maintain some liquidity to meet his future needs.

In this case the Family Limited Partnership combined with the Asset Protection Trust was used to enhance Peter's negotiating leverage with the bank. By removing the cash into a protected position, the bank was forced to focus on the apartment house as the security for the loan and the cash was no longer a tempting target. The transaction did not raise any fraudulent conveyance issues because Peter was still solvent after the transfer of the cash.

In many situations involving negotiations with

lenders concerning rescheduling payments and similar matters, it may be possible to significantly improve your bargaining position by protecting liquid assets through the asset protection structure. Naturally, caution must be exercised to insure that the transaction does not violate any of the fraudulent transfer laws.

WHAT ARE THE OBJECTIVES OF AN ASSET PROTECTION PLAN?

Sound Legal Foundation

Any asset protection plan prepared by a responsible attorney must be based upon a sound legal foundation of established principals of law. An appropriate plan does not involve hiding or concealing assets or otherwise attempting to defraud creditors. A properly constructed asset protection plan will allow you to achieve your objectives while fully and truthfully disclosing all of your financial circumstances.

Discouraging Litigation

An asset protection plan is designed to discourage a potential lawsuit before it begins. In the ordinary course of litigation, the attorney for the plaintiff will want to make sure that sufficient assets of the defendant can be reached if the litigation is successful. This is especially true when the attorney is working for a contingent fee. Accordingly, prior to commencing a lawsuit, the plaintiff's attorney will perform a financial investigation of your assets, seeking to locate any real estate, bank accounts or other valuable property. If you have substantial, reachable assets the lawsuit will go forward. If the investigation reveals that your assets are not in a form that can be seized, only the most self destructive plaintiff would incur the expense of proceeding with the case.

Allowing Access to Funds Prior to Trial

In many types of litigation the plaintiff can obtain from the court a *Pre-Judgment Writ of Attachment* or a restraining order effectively freezing all of your funds pending the outcome of the case. This is often the single most potent weapon available to the plaintiff. Without access to funds to meet your business and personal expenses you will not be able to survive financially during the lawsuit. This tactic will usually force you to enter into an unfavorable settlement regardless of the merits of your defense.

The objective of an asset protection plan is to make sure that your property cannot be tied up in this manner in the event of litigation. An appropriate plan should be designed to keep real-estate assets free of attachments and liens and should allow you to maintain undisturbed access to your funds during the litigation process.

Access to Funds After Judgment

If you are sued and there is a judgment against you, your real estate, and bank accounts will be effectively frozen. You will not be able to sell or refinance your property or use your funds to meet your needs and obligations. Assets which have been properly transferred into the Family Limited Partnership or Asset Protection Trust will not be subject to the Judgment Lien. You will retain your ability to deal with your property and bank accounts. The effect of the plan will be to dramatically increase your negotiating leverage and your ability to dictate the terms of any potential settlement.

QUESTIONS AND ANSWERS

APPENDIX

C

Ease of Operation

An asset protection plan should be easy and convenient for you to use and understand. After the plan has been established, you should be able to deal with your property without difficult or burdensome restrictions.

No Loss of Control

An asset protection plan must allow you to maintain continued control and enjoyment over your property. A plan that requires you to place your valuable assets under the direction and management of a third party will not be appealing to even the most sophisticated individuals.

Consistent with Estate Plan

If you have an existing estate plan, such as a will or a living trust, the asset protection plan must be consistent with these arrangements. If you have not yet created any estate planning documents, the asset protection plan must be designed to minimize or avoid estate taxes, avoid a costly and time consuming probate procedure and pass your property in accordance with your wishes.

Protection of Family Assets

Above all else, the asset protection plan must in fact accomplish its primary purpose of safely insulating and preserving family assets from any kind of attack. If a structure is not properly established within the appropriate time period and with the correct mechanisms in place, the hoped for asset protection features will not be available.

WHO NEEDS ASSET PROTECTION?

Everyone who has something to lose needs asset protection. If you own a home or a business or if you are trying to put together a nest egg for your retirement you will want to protect against financial disaster.

CAN I USE A CORPORATION TO PROTECT MY ASSETS?

A corporation is ordinarily not considered to be an effective device for protecting one's assets from lawsuits. This is so because the shares of corporate stock are easily reachable by a creditor. Once the creditor has seized the shares, he becomes a shareholder in the corporation and may be permitted to legally dissolve the corporation. In many states, a shareholder owning 30% or more of the stock in the corporation can petition a court to dissolve the company. Therefore, if you wish to use a corporation for asset protection, you cannot own a percentage of the corporate shares that will allow the creditor to take those shares and dissolve the corporation.

Asset protection can be achieved if a significant percentage of the corporate shares are placed in the Family Limited Partnership. Unless the creditor is able to prove a fraudulent conveyance, he will not be able to reach those shares. If the remaining shares are not sufficient to allow a creditor to legally dissolve the corporation, the result is that a high level of asset protection will have been achieved.

Remember, although a corporation is usually a good vehicle for conducting an active business, it is generally not recommended for holding passive, investment type assets. Holding investment assets in a corporation will often produce unwanted tax consequences. These type of assets should be held in the Family Limited Partnership.

WILL I BE PROTECTED FROM LAWSUITS IF I GIVE ALL MY PROPERTY TO MY WIFE?

A gift of property which is not a fraudulent conveyance will be effective in removing that property from the husband's potential creditors. However, if after the gift the husband continues to enjoy the use of the property, a court may find that the gift was not really a gift. For example, if the husband transfers title to the family house to his wife and continues to live in the house, a court could find that the transfer created an implied trust for the benefit of both husband and wife. An implied trust would be found if the court determined that there was an agreement or understanding between the husband and wife that the property would be held by the wife for their joint benefit. Such a finding would negate the gift and would allow the creditors of the husband to reach his interest in the house.

Gifts which are made to a spouse, in trust, may eliminate this problem. An express trust, one whose terms are fully written, is more likely to withstand attack than an outright gift.

SHOULD MY BUSINESS BE INCORPORATED?

A corporation can provide a meaningful limitation on one's personal liability and should be used to conduct any type of business. If a corporation is properly maintained and the corporate formalities are followed, personal liability for many types of activities will be eliminated. Although lenders, landlords and many suppliers will often require personal guarantees by the shareholders of any corporate obligations, personal liability for other types of contracts can be significantly diminished. The drawbacks to incorporation involve the additional accounting and legal expenses, annual state filing requirements, and potential corporate income taxes. These costs must be weighed against the benefits of avoiding personal lawsuits and liability for many corporate obligations.

HOW DOES THE FAMILY LIMITED PARTNERSHIP WORK?

The Family Limited Partnership is an extremely useful device for accomplishing a variety of asset protection objectives. This type of arrangement is so effective because it allows you to maintain control and management over family assets without having an interest that can be seized by a creditor. Assets which have been transferred to the FLP cannot be reached by a creditor unless he can demonstrate that the transfer was a fraudulent conveyance.

Rather than reaching the assets in the FLP the creditor is limited to the remedy known as the charging order. A charging order is a court ordered direction that any distributions to be paid to the debtor partner must instead be paid to the judgment creditor. The judgment creditor does not become a substituted limited partner, nor does he acquire any rights to management of partnership affairs. He has no right to interfere in the activities of the partnership. The effect of this strategy is to dramatically alter the relationship between the debtor partner and the judgment creditor. Rather than having the ability to levy and executed directly upon the debtor's assets, the creditor must now go through the charging order procedure. If the partnership does not make any distributions during the term of the charging order, the creditor will not receive any payments. Because the creditor cannot reach the assets of the partnership and must wait for distributions, family assets will be successfully protected.

When the Family Limited Partnership is used in conjunction with a domestic or Asset Protection Trust, which holds the limited partnership interests in the FLP an even more significant level of protection is achieved. Limited Partnership interests held by the trust will not be subject to a charging order or foreclosure because these interests are no longer "owned" by the debtor partner.

ARE FAMILY LIMITED PARTNERSHIPS DIFFICULT TO USE?

The Family Limited Partnership is a very easy and convenient way to hold and manage one's assets. We advise our clients to keep one bank account outside of the partnership in order to pay household expenses. Any surplus is then transferred into the partnership account. The only inconvenience is the requirement that federal and state income tax returns be prepared for the partnership, which results in additional tax preparation fees.

IS IT DIFFICULT TO MOVE PROPERTY IN OR OUT OF THE FAMILY LIMITED PARTNERSHIP?

The general partners always have full legal authority to execute all documents and deeds on behalf of the partnership without the approval or consent of the limited partners.

IF I USE A FAMILY LIMITED PARTNERSHIP, DO I STILL NEED A LIVING TRUST?

A Family Limited Partnership can be used in conjunction with a revocable living trust. As stated, although the living trust does not provide any asset protection benefits, it is useful in accomplishing certain estate planning objectives. A funded living trust will avoid probate on family assets and will provide for the disposition of the property upon the death of a spouse. However, because the assets of the living trust will be exposed to a creditor, upon the death of a spouse, most people prefer to use an Asset Protection Trust which will accomplish the same objectives of the living trust, without exposing the assets to the claims of a creditor.

IF I USE A FAMILY LIMITED PARTNERSHIP, CAN I CANCEL MY LIABILITY INSURANCE?

We do not recommend that our clients cancel any existing liability policies which they have. However, it is worth exploring whether the amount of the coverage can be reduced. One reason for maintaining the liability coverage is that you want the insurance company to pay for your legal defense in the event that you are sued. If you do not have insurance coverage, you will have to pay for your legal fees out of your own pocket. An alternative to paying your own legal costs would be to do nothing to defend the lawsuit, permitting the plaintiff to take a judgment by default in the case. Although partnership assets will be protected from the judgment creditor, it will be possible for the creditor to garnish wages, attach future income, or restrict access to partnership funds through the charging order procedure. If you have an arguable legal defense to the plaintiff's suit, it is better to have your day in court and attempt to win the lawsuit in order to avoid the consequences of having a judgment against you.

Although dropping coverage entirely would not be prudent, it may be possible to reduce the amount of the liability coverage. For example, a client of ours with the net worth of approximately $2,000,000 maintained liability insurance of $1,000,000. After we created the Family Limited Partnership structure, he reduced his liability coverage to $100,000. This resulted in a substantial annual premium reduction. The logic of that decision is that a plaintiff's attorney, performing an asset search on our client would not discover any assets owned by him. Because of this, the plaintiff's attorney would be likely to settle for the $100,000 policy limit rather than attempting to go to trial and obtain a larger judgment without any assurance that the larger judgment could be collected. Under the proper circumstance, a reduction in the amount of coverage would be warranted and could be accomplished through the use of the proper asset protection strategies.

IS A TRANSFER TO A FAMILY LIMITED PARTNERSHIP A FRAUDULENT CONVEYANCE?

A fraudulent conveyance is a transfer which is intended to hinder, delay or defraud a creditor from the collection of his debt. A transfer which is made with an actual intent to defraud a creditor or which renders the transferor insolvent will be considered to be a fraudulent conveyance. A transfer which is a fraudulent conveyance can be set aside by the creditor. In determining whether you have made a fraudulent conveyance, the court will focus on both an objective and a subjective test. The objective test is based upon whether the transfer rendered you insolvent. Generally, insolvency means an inability to meet current debts as they become due. Also, the court will use a balance sheet test to determine if after the transfer, your liabilities exceeded your assets.

The subjective test is based upon your intent at the time of the transfer. Under this test, the business purposes for establishing the Family Limited Partnership will be scrutinized. For example, if a significant motivation for establishing the Family Limited Partnership was to accomplish various estate planning objectives, such as providing a mechanism for giving gifts to one's children, a creditor would have a difficult time establishing a fraudulent intent in the creation of a partnership.

Ultimately the issue will really come down to one of timing. Was the transfer made in such close proximity to a lawsuit or a judgment that an intent to defraud is the only credible finding? Clearly, the greater the distance between a transfer and a lawsuit, the stronger the argument that the predominant motivation was not fraudulent as to a particular creditor.

ARE FAMILY LIMITED PARTNERSHIPS USEFUL FOR ESTATE PLANNING?

Family Limited Partnerships fit in beautifully with traditional estate planning objectives. The primary objective of most estate planning strategies is to minimize estate taxes. A widely used technique for reducing estate taxes involves a lifetime gift-giving program to family members in amounts which fall within the annual gift tax exclusion of $10,000 per year to each donee. For a variety of reasons, gifts of cash or transfers of fractional interests in deeds to real property are usually not favored as gift-giving techniques.

The Family Limited Partnership provides an easy and convenient mechanism for making gifts to family members. Each year a limited partnership interest, valued less than the amount of the annual exclusion can be transferred to family members. A limited partnership interest gives the donee no right to participate in management and control of partnership affairs, so the gift-giver effectively retains control over the property in the partnership. At the same time, if the partnership is properly structured, the value of the gifted partnership interests will be excluded from the donor's estate at the time of his death and estate taxes will be avoided on the amount of the gifted interests.

These techniques for reducing estate taxes will assume even greater significance if Congress goes forward with the plan to reduce the lifetime exemption from $600,000 to $200,000. This change would cause a husband and wife with a combined estate over $400,000 to incur estate taxes when passing property down to their children. The Family Limited Partnership arrangement would provide an excellent means for reducing estate taxes through annual gifts of limited partnership interests, without any loss of control of the family assets.

HOW ARE DOMESTIC TRUSTS USED FOR ASSET PROTECTION?

One popular approach is to establish a domestic trust for the purpose of holding the limited partnership interests in the FLP. The trust does not hold any assets directly, other than the limited partnership interests.

Under the usual arrangement the husband and wife may be trustees and the children are named as beneficiaries. The parents cannot be the beneficiaries of the trust because the law of every state allows a creditor to reach the assets of the trust if the parents retain an interest in a trust which they have created. Also, the trust must be irrevocable. That is, the parents cannot retain any power to alter, amend, or revoke the trust at any time.

In order to avoid any liability for Federal gift taxes, the transfer to the trust can be structured as an *incomplete gift*. Although the transfer is effective for creditor protection purposes, if the parents retain certain powers to alter the interests of the beneficiaries, the gift will not be considered to be complete under Federal tax law. As a result, the transfer will not create any gift tax exposure for the parents. Instead, the amount in the trust will be included in the parents estate upon their death and will remain subject to estate tax liability. Similarly, for income tax purposes the trust will be treated as a *grantor trust.* All income of the trust will be reported on the parent's tax return in the same manner as if the transfer had never occurred.

HOW DOES THE ASSET PROTECTION TRUST WORK?

A popular alternative to the domestic trust is an Asset Protection Trust. A trust which is established under the laws of a foreign country provides certain advantages which cannot be achieved with a domestic trust. Certain countries such as the Cook Islands have laws that are much more favorable to asset protection then the laws in the United States. By creating a trust under the laws of one of these jurisdictions an individual can obtain greater protection and flexibility then that which is available for trusts formed under U.S. law.

In using the Asset Protection Trust the individual does not sacrifice any degree of immediate control and access to his property. *All bank accounts and real estate remain in the FLP. The only asset transferred to the trust is the interest in the FLP.* The individual, as general partner of the FLP, retains total authority over his property.

If at any point there is an attack upon this structure by a creditor, the FLP can distribute its liquid assets and personal property to an offshore account that has been established in the name of the trust. This feature provides the ultimate protection for family assets since this account will not be subject to the jurisdiction of a U.S. Court. Once assets have been safely relocated under the protection of the laws of that country, recovery of the funds by the creditor becomes unlikely.

The tax rules governing these kind of trusts are identical to those concerning the domestic trust. For both income tax and estate tax law, the Asset Protection Trust is ignored by the IRS. Properly structured, there are no gift tax consequences to the arrangement and all income of the trust is reported directly on the return of the settlor.

CAN YOU PROVIDE A SUMMARY OF HOW ALL OF THE PIECES OF THE ASSET PROTECTION PLAN FIT TOGETHER?

Here is an example of how the asset protection plan operates from a practical standpoint. James and Mary Prudence have accumulated a nest-egg of $200,000 for their retirement. Together they own and operate a fast food restaurant. They want to make certain that their savings are protected no matter what happens from any type of lawsuit or claim.

They form the Prudence Family Limited Partnership. John and Mary are the General Partners, each owning a one percent interest. They transfer the ninety-eight percent limited partnership interest to the Asset Protection Trust. They are both Trustees of the Trust, and the Trust Company in the Cook Islands serves as an additional Trustee. James and Mary are the beneficiaries of the Trust.

James and Mary open a bank account or a brokerage account in the name of the Prudence Family Limited Partnership. This is a very simple matter that takes only a few minutes. The signatories on the account are James and Mary. They maintain a regular checking account, outside of the Partnership, which they use to pay their normal monthly expenses. Any surplus goes into the Partnership account. If they need to use any of the amounts in the Partnership they can simply write a check on that account.

This arrangement does not have any income tax or gift tax consequences. All dividend or interest income earned by the Partnership is reported on James and Mary's income tax return. There are no tax savings or disadvantages.

Similarly, there are no gift tax consequences. Since James and Mary have full control over their property, there are no gift tax implications to this set-up.

Now let's see what happens if there is ever someone who is thinking about suing James or Mary. As we have seen, the plaintiff's lawyer will want to know whether it is worth his time and money to pursue James and Mary in a lawsuit. When he performs an asset search, he is unable to locate any property whatsoever in the name of James and Mary, since they have previously transferred their property to their Family Limited Partnership. It is very unlikely that he would proceed at this point.

But let's say that the lawsuit is filed and James and Mary lose. Now what happens?

Remember, after the lawsuit the collection process begins with a Debtor's Examination, with detailed questions concerning the sources of income and the location of assets. Clearly, if James and Mary had *not* transferred their assets into the Family Limited Partnership, the judgment creditor would simply have levied on their bank accounts and taken all of their retirement savings. There would be no room to negotiate and no leverage to attempt to work out a deal or a payment schedule. Under normal circumstances, a creditor with a judgment holds all of the cards.

Now the situation is quite different. First of all, James and Mary will truthfully answer all of the questions in the judgment debtor exam. They will state that they own a one percent interest in the Family Limited Partnership and that they are the beneficiaries of the Trust. Again, the purpose of the arrangement is not to hide or conceal assets from a creditor. The program allows you to answer all questions truthfully and completely.

Now that the plaintiff knows how the assets are held, what does he do? Will he be able to collect on his judgment? The plaintiff would like to seize the cash in the Family Limited Partnership but he cannot do that. As we have discussed, a creditor is not permitted to reach the assets of a partnership to satisfy the debts of a partner.

What about the Limited Partnership interests held by the trust? If the plaintiff can seize those interests he would at least have something for his efforts. But, fortunately, the limited partnership interests cannot be seized because they are held by a valid, legal trust, outside of the jurisdiction of a U.S court.

What is the next move? Could the plaintiff go to the Cook Islands and enforce the judgment there? Again, the answer is no. The law of the Cook Islands specifically provides that a judgment of a foreign court cannot be enforced in the Cook Islands. The Limited Partnership interests are safely protected.

At this point the creditor will certainly be willing to settle for pennies on the dollar. James and Mary can now choose to settle on their terms, if they wish. Or they can choose not to pay any settlement at all.

As a practical matter, James and Mary have clearly produced a very successful result. They have shielded their valuable assets and guaranteed that their retirement nest-egg is secure.

ABOUT THE AUTHORS

ROBERT J. MINTZ

Robert J. Mintz has been practicing law in the Los Angeles area since 1979. He received his Bachelor of Arts degree from the University of California, Berkeley, in 1974 and his law degree from the University of San Diego in 1978. He also received a Masters of Law degree in Taxation from Boston University in 1979. Mr. Mintz has lectured, Published and taught in the fields of taxation, estate planning and asset protection. Mr. Mintz maintains law offices in Los Angeles and San Diego and devotes his practice exclusively to asset protection matters.

JAMES J. RUBENS

James J. Rubens received his undergraduate degree from Northwestern University in 1971 and his law degree from Georgetown School of Law in 1976. He has been practicing law in Los Angeles since 1977. Mr. Rubens practice is concentrated in the areas of real estate, business and asset protection.

FREE
ASSET PROTECTION
KIT

If you would like more information on the topic of Asset Protection please write or call us at the address below and we will be happy to speak with you or send you a free Asset Protection Kit containing the latest material on the subject.

Robert J. Mintz
1201 Camino Del Mar Suite 203
San Diego, CA 92014
(800) 223-4291